MUSEUM FÜR GESTALTUNG ZÜRICH

KING STAG

CARLO GOZZI'S TRAGICOMEDY IN A STAGING FOR MARIONETTES BY SOPHIE TAEUBER-ARP, RENÉ MORAX, AND WERNER WOLFF

SCHEIDEGGER & SPIESS

CLEAR THE STAGE

WELCOME!

N o sooner has the scholarly Freudanalytikus of Vienna arrived in the fair city of Serendippo than its long-entrenched status quo and seemingly intractable situations there begin to shift. The year is 1918 and the true scene of the action, where his "loyal pupil" Doctor Oedipus Complex is expecting him, turns out to be Zurich; the clue is in the mention of certain illustrious addresses and other local references. The great magician's arrival sets in motion all manner of romantic entanglements, unseemly quarrels, and infighting over the reigning King Deramo's choice of bride. We even get to see a magic statue mobilized as a psychoanalytical tool for judging the various candidates. The "King Stag" of the title proves to be a bestial changeling, that being the guise in which the king finally has to face up to the true nature of his power-hungry prime minister Tartaglia. If the impending tragedy is averted, then it is thanks ultimately to the discoverer of the "Urlibido," Freudanalytikus, who in a nod to the two great psychoanalysts of the age urges the audience to "be young [*jung*] and of good cheer [*freudig*]."

The puppet play *King Stag*, penned by playwrights René Morax and Werner Wolff, is published here in full for the first time, to complete and enhance Sophie Taeuber-Arp's already famous avant-garde puppet ensemble.[1]

The 1918 staging of *King Stag* was commissioned by what was then the Gewerbeschule (Trade School) and is now the Zurich University of the Arts. Alfred Altherr, the director of that institution and co-founder of the Swiss Werkbund, had launched a new puppet theater for the forthcoming Werkbund exhibition in Zurich. There were to be nine plays for which he needed to engage authors and designers to create the figures and sets. Morax and Wolff were among the playwrights approached and they delivered not just their own texts but also an adaptation of Carlo Gozzi's

From left to right: Erika Schlegel-Taeuber, Carl Gustav Jung, unknown person, Anna Stauffacher-Nistelweck, and Sophie Taeuber-Arp at the Carnival party of the Psychological Club Zurich, 1920s

commedia dell'arte fairy tale *Il re cervo* of 1762. Besides being a turbulent tragicomedy about love and deception, this modern retelling of the work also references the psychoanalysis and includes allusions to Dada as well as other topical issues.

The sets and puppets for this modern version of *King Stag* were designed by Sophie Taeuber-Arp, who had been teaching textile design at the Gewerbeschule since 1916. She had come to know about psychoanalysis through her sister, Erika Schlegel, who had undergone psychoanalysis with Carl Gustav Jung and was a member of Zurich's Psychological Club as well as its librarian. A photo of a Carnival party at the Psychological Club in the 1920s shows Jung in an intimate setting, armed with a tobacco pipe, and surrounded by no fewer than four women. Jung himself, like the Taeuber sisters Erika and Sophie, is wearing an eccentric headdress. If *King Stag*'s parody of him as the inept, stumpy-legged, and priggish Doctor Oedipus Complex had caused him any offense, evidently he has long since overcome and forgotten it [fig. 1].

Taeuber-Arp conceived her figures' characters based on Morax and Wolff's updated script and supplied detailed production drawings so that they could be made quickly, just as she intended. The sketches show the joints as exposed eye bolts as well as other elements that would later be dropped. Among these were the eyes and mouths of the Guards' many different heads as well as Tartaglia's relatively plain headdress, which in formal terms was to have echoed King Deramo's helmet ornament, and sheet-metal backplate, later replaced by a mantle [figs. 2–3].

Taeuber-Arp was rigorous about molding the figures' bodies and facial features to their roles. Whereas the titled characters are all clad in subdued shades, the three servants Truffaldin, Brighella, and Smeraldina, who provide most of the comic relief, are defined by bright and bold primary colors. The eloquent

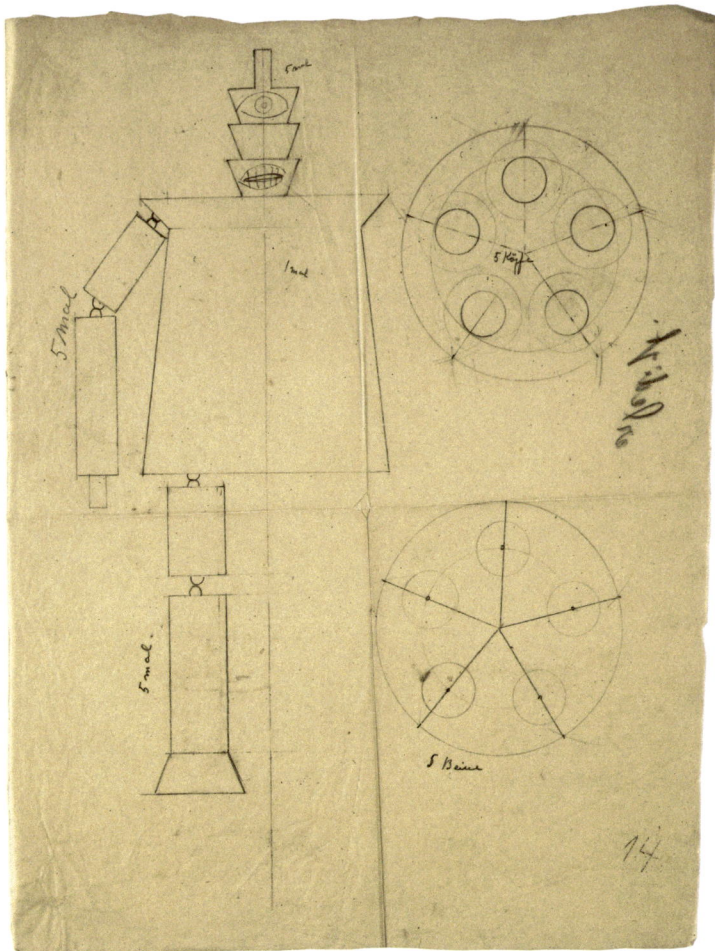

[fig. 2]   Sophie Taeuber-Arp, design for the figure of the
            Guards (*King Stag*), pencil on tracing paper,
            51.2 × 40 cm, 1918

Sophie Taeuber-Arp, study for the figure of
Tartaglia (*King Stag*), pencil on tracing paper,
51 × 26.5 cm, 1918

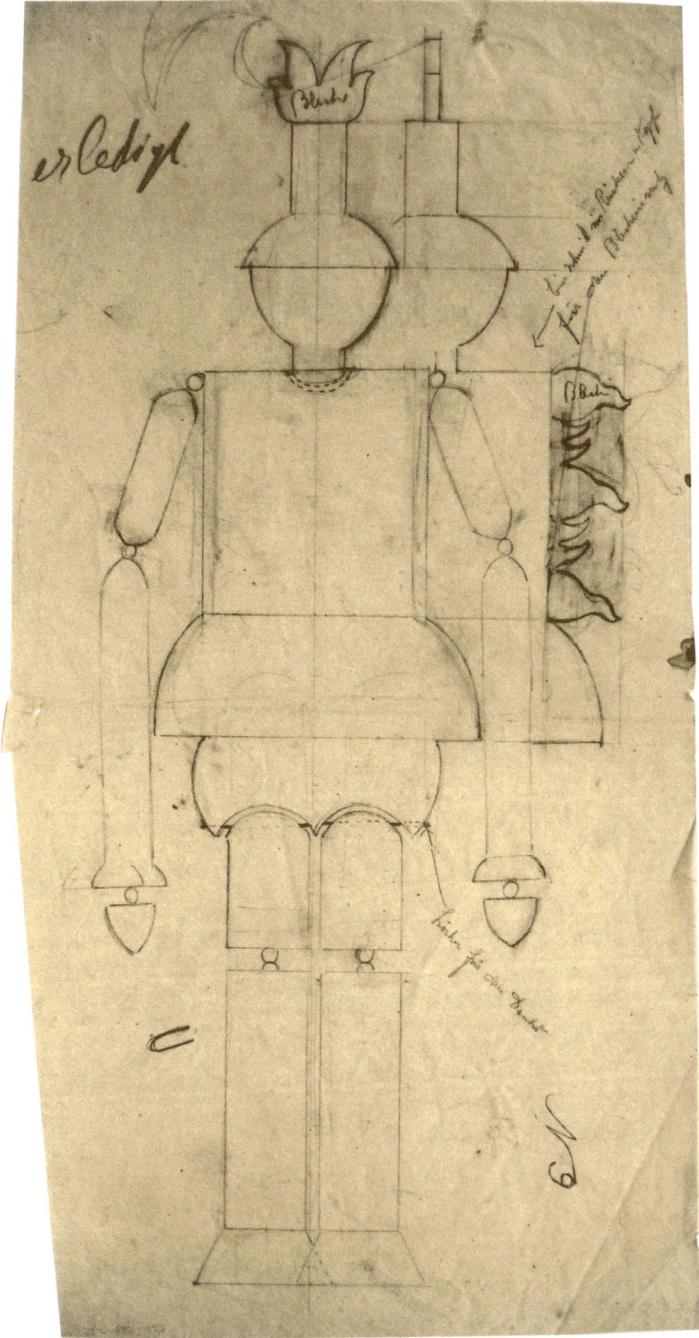

Freudanalytikus underscores his theories by gesticulating with his excessively long arms and making full use of a segmented body that can be twisted in all directions; the garrulous Smeraldina, by contrast, has such an unshakable faith in her brazenly showcased physical charms that she is quite barefaced about her intentions. The blue-trunked tree, as a *pars pro toto* of the Burghölzli forest, serves to fire the imagination, and as a silent witness throws the jockeying for power played out in front of the geometric backdrops even more sharply into relief. The figures' dance-like movements carry echoes of the circles in which Taeuber-Arp still moved, even as she worked towards establishing herself as an independent artist.

The painstaking execution of the marionettes was organized by fellow teacher Carl Fischer. As a teacher of woodcarving at the Gewerbeschule right up to the 1940s, he would eventually carve all the marionettes belonging to the Schweizerisches Marionettentheater (Swiss Puppet Theater), later the Zürcher Marionetten. Lacking the necessary lathing skills, however, he contracted out both the unusual task of turning Taeuber-Arp's puppets and the work of making the brass elements. Once the parts had been made, he took care of their assembly, while Taeuber-Arp herself endowed the figures with their poetic and richly referential painted liveries and textile embellishments [fig. 4].

The seventeen marionettes for *King Stag*, along with what few props had survived and the three stage sets, whose current whereabouts are unknown, entered the collection of the Kunstgewerbemuseum (Museum of Arts and Crafts, now the Museum für Gestaltung Zürich) as early as October 1919. Today, the marionettes can be viewed in the archive. Replicas made for exhibition purposes have been loaned to museums all over the world from Basel, London, Paris, and Madrid to Oslo, Washington, New York, and Taipei. In all these cities, excited visitors have been able to study them and marvel at them, whether in the context of avant-garde art, the Dada movement, the Lebensreform movement on Monte Verità, or even, at least in the case of the puppet Guards, as part of a robot exhibition. Solo exhibitions drawing on Taeuber-Arp's whole oeuvre have further added to her fame and at the same time have also increased interest in the marionettes.

The last time the puppets were used in a performance was in 1965, when Hans Hiller staged Carlo Gozzi's *Il re cervo* at the puppet theater in St. Gallen. In June 1993, the Zürcher Puppen Theater (Zurich Puppet Theater, now the Theater Stadelhofen) put on a production of the Morax and Wolff version of *King Stag* using a specially made set of puppets and reconstructed backdrops. To commemorate the fiftieth anniversary of Taeuber-Arp's death, some members of the Schauspielakademie (School of Dramatic Arts) also manipulated the puppets and lent them their voices [fig. 5].

Despite being made of wood, the figures remain full of vigor and vitality and invariably touch a nerve, even as museum exhibits. The interest taken in them by art historians and researchers in other fields has thus remained consistently high. Designed as stand-alone objects that are both fleet of foot and fully articulated, each is endowed with an unusual and open-ended range of movements that even today invites further inquiry, including some recent projects in the field of film and digital media. In *La Dada* of 2016, the Zurich-based director Anka Schmid had the puppets shadowed by human dancers, while in 2025, students of "Digital Play" at Zurich University of the Arts and of the "Laboratory for Experimental Museology (eM+)" at the École Polytechnique Fédérale in Lausanne used the marionettes to ascertain how digital tools enable their own forms of artistic expression.

[fig. 5] Rehearsals for the reconstruction of *King Stag*,
camera team in front of the stage set
"King's Cabinet," Zürcher Puppen Theater, 1992

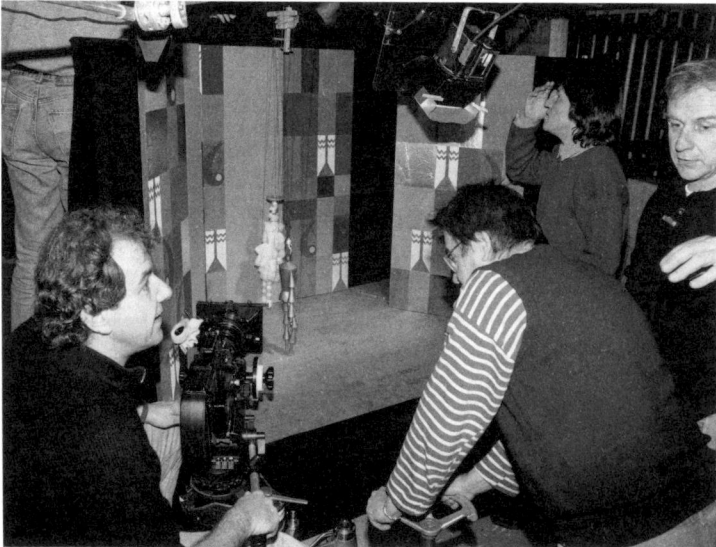

At the textual level, too, the play opens up a wide range of analytical contexts, which doubtless explains the large number of requests to view the script that have been received in recent years. The 150th anniversary of the birth of Jung being celebrated in 2025 has prompted still more interest in *King Stag* and its contemporary take on psychoanalysis. The extent to which an average audience in Zurich in 1918 would have been familiar with what Freud and Jung were actually doing and their influence on the cantonal psychiatric hospital known as the Burghölzli is impossible to say. Perhaps they simply found the play amusing. The fact that Freud left Vienna to visit Zurich a second time five years after his first visit provided exactly the same premise as that underlying the eighteenth-century drama *Il re cervo*, in which the magician Durandarte returns to Serendippo after an absence of five years.

The authors of the essays in this publication each approached *King Stag* from the vantage point of their own field of expertise. In the "Program Booklet," the scientific collaborators Julia Klinner and Sophie Grossmann, together with the author of this text and curator of the Decorative Arts Collection, present the exact role and characteristics of each of the puppets in turn, quoting some of their lines and, where relevant, referencing their formal affinities with commedia dell'arte characters and Gozzi's fairy-tale play of 1762.

The contributors to "Applause" view the play *King Stag* from four different perspectives. As an art historian, Medea Hoch takes a deep dive into the avant-garde interest in puppet plays more generally, affording readers an insight into Alfred Altherr's promotion of a Schweizerisches Marionettentheater and the specific steps taken by the Marionettes Committee in its choice of authors and designers. Following the history of the genre back to its roots, she draws on the numerous contemporary press reviews and enthusiastic reception of the piece by fellow artists to give us a sense of how exciting Taeuber-Arp's work was felt to be.

Hana Ribi, a theater studies specialist and expert in figural theater, explains the significance of the commedia dell'arte to the avant-garde artists of the early twentieth century, taking Gozzi's *Il re cervo* as her starting point. What made that work so special, she argues, was the way Gozzi combined a typically Italian tradition based on improvisation, pantomime, dance, slapstick, and coarse language with characters from fairy tales. Also examined here is how his text came to be revised and the influence on that process of Edward Gordon Craig, Adolphe Appia, and other exponents of "New Theater," including those, like Morax, who were active in French-speaking Switzerland's progressive theater scene.

The professor of dance studies Christina Thurner discusses the spatio-dynamic properties of the marionettes' dynamic, in relation to avant-garde dance of the 1910s, of which Taeuber-Arp herself was an active practitioner. The author also elucidates how Taeuber-Arp's own knowledge of dance and movement influenced the conception of her figures and above all their possession of what Rudolf von Laban called "dancing sense."

As a curator at the Arp Museum Bahnhof Rolandseck, Astrid von Asten sheds light on the place of the *King Stag* marionettes in Taeuber-Arp's oeuvre as a whole. The puppets, she notes, exemplify Taeuber-Arp's practice of working with the properties intrinsic to her materials, even as she tried to square the circle of teaching traditional craft techniques at the Gewerbeschule while at the same time being active in avant-garde circles. The marionettes for *King Stag* were created in parallel to Taeuber-Arp's *Têtes Dada*, while some of the design elements for the puppet theater would recur in other contexts, such as the in-

26

terior designs created for the Café Aubette and dance hall in Strasbourg.

This publication reunites the figures and script of *King Stag* for the first time. Writing in the last year of the First World War, the playwrights Morax and Wolff managed to turn an eighteenth-century plot into a witty blend of invention and intrigue, using a language that is as full of vows of undying love as it is of colorful curses, to say nothing of references to local issues such as stranded deserters, usurers, Dadaists, the threat of a general strike, and the rise of psycho-analysis. Taeuber-Arp, for her part, staged her marionettes' characters with great care and artistic empathy; they are all dancers by nature, whose nerves are very much on edge as they watch a tense and intense era unfold.

1   Carlo Gozzi, *König Hirsch*, dramaturgically revised by René Morax, trans. from the French and expanded by Werner Wolff, typescript, 1918. Museum für Gestaltung Zürich, Decorative Arts Collection/ZHdK. The English translation of the original German typescript, *King Stag*, can be found on pp. 129–183.

PROGRAM
BOOKLET

Schweizer. Werkbund-Ausstellung
Zürich 1918

Marionetten-
Theater

Tägliche Vorstellungen:
3 Uhr, 5 Uhr, 8½ Uhr 🙪 Programm
in den Tageszeitungen 🙪 Preise: 3 Fr.,
2 Fr., 1 Fr., 50 Rp. 🙪 Kinder können mit
einem Theaterbillett auch die Ausstellung
besuchen 🙪 Schulen 25 Rp. für jedes Kind
Für Gesellschaften Sonder-Vorstellungen
mit ermässigten Preisen 🙪 Alle Plätze
nummeriert 🙪 Vorverkauf: Kuoni,
Bahnhofplatz u. Hauptkasse Ausstellung
🙪 🙪 Telephon Hottingen 65.87 🙪 🙪

Swiss Werkbund, program of the puppet play
König Hirsch (King Stag) performed as part of the Werkbund
exhibition in Zurich, 22.8 × 18 cm, 1918

Schweizer. Werkbund-Ausstellung Zürich 1918

Marionetten-Theater

König Hirsch

Ein tragikomisches Märchen in 3 Akten von Gozzi

In der Übersetzung und Bearbeitung
von René Morax und Werner Wolff

Personen:

Dr. Komplex . . . .
Freudanalytikus . . . .
Deramo, König von Serendippo .
Tartaglia, Minister . . . .
Pantalon, Minister . . . .
Clarissa, Tochter des Tartaglia . .
Angela, Tochter des Pantalon . .
Leander, Sohn des Pantalon . . .
Brighella, des Königs Mundschenk .
Smeraldina, seine Schwester . . . .
Truffaldin, der Vogelfänger . . . .
Wachen . . . .

Ort der Handlung im königlichen Palaste zu Serendippo
und im nahen Walde Roneisloppe.

Dekorationen und Figurinen von Sophie H. Taeuber, S. W. B. Zürich.

NEUE ZÜRCHER ZEITUNG, ZÜRICH.

THE ENSEMBLE

Stage set "King's Cabinet," *King Stag*, 1918. Sophie Taeuber-Arp's notes read as follows: "In many shades of red, mainly cinnabar. The light patches are silvered. At first, these flecks of silver are all that can be seen in the dim light

of the transfiguration scene. Then the room begins to softly glow, eventually becoming a radiant red. The statue (the magic gift) in the background is wood with conspicuous faux marbling in dark gray against a red background."

Stage set "The King's Antechamber," *King Stag*, 1918.
Sophie Taeuber-Arp's notes read as follows:

"Shaded pink. Gap at rear a radiant bright blue. In front a blue vase with feathery flowers with red and black fabric stalks."

Stage set "In the Forest," *King Stag*, 1918.
Sophie Taeuber-Arp's notes read as follows: "Olive green and yellow.
The wide stripe on the left symbolizes falling water and is blue.

2 trees and 2 bushes gr[ee]n with green woolen leaves.
The two stags white with brass antlers. 1 stag is the king transfigured
in the magic forest."

Stage set "King's Cabinet" with final scene, *King Stag*, 1918

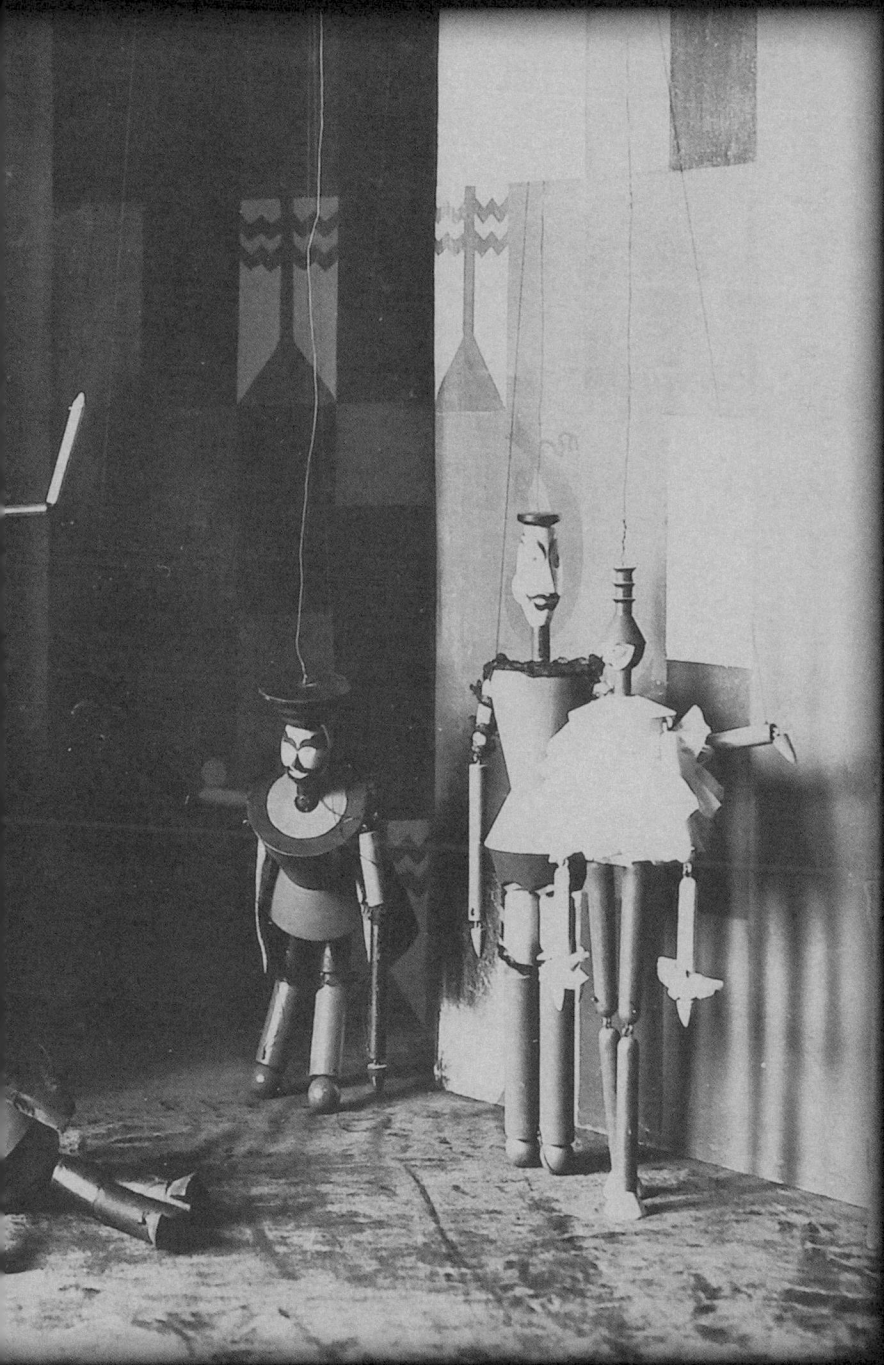

Here we are at Sechseläutenplatz in Zurich, the site of the *Raumkunst* exhibition to be staged by the Swiss Werkbund founded in 1913. The exhibition, which is to run from May 18 to September 15, 1918 showcases and offers for sale "objectively well made and accordingly priced work" in numerous furnished showrooms. Zurich's newly founded puppet theater, the Schweizerisches Marionettentheater, is part of the show that occupies a grand building with a colonnaded courtyard. The building was designed by the architect and then director of the Gewerbeschule (Trade School) Alfred Altherr, who was passionate about puppet theater, as a platform for artistic all-overs. The realistic depictions of stags and deer in the decorative facade paintings by Paul Bodmer give us a feel for the prevailing taste.

There are daily performances at 3 and 5 in the afternoon and 8.30 in the evening, and on Sundays a matinée at 11. The theater seats 172 spectators who get to see naturalistic marionettes in delightful little costumes performing on a stage that is 2.5 meters wide.

But the program also includes two plays that each feature an avant-garde ensemble: *La boîte à joujoux*, with stage sets and figurines by Otto Morach, and *King Stag,* the designs for which are the work of Sophie Taeuber-Arp. Morach is an artist who also teaches at the Gewerbeschule Zürich. Influenced by Futurism, he paints his stylized, carved figures in shaded primary colors and has them act as finely modeled sculptures. Sophie Taeuber-Arp, a teacher at the same school, goes a stage further in her adaptation of *King Stag:* in a radical departure from naturalism, her ensemble consisting of stylistically coherent, abstract figures breaks with every convention of the genre.

he lights are dimmed and the adults in the audience lean back in their seats, while, behind the scenes, the puppet masters have their fingers firmly on the control bars. A spotlight scans the darkness, eventually landing on a cone-shaped figure sporting red and yellow stripes, large spectacles, and flamboyant brass plumes on his head. He introduces himself as Doctor Oedipus Complex, a "loyal pupil" of the great Freudanalytikus. This provokes the first laughs. So this is going to be a drama about psychoanalysis! Despite being called *King Stag*? Well, this could be fun! Let us follow Doctor Oedipus Complex and take a close

"Ladies and
gentlemen,
honored guests,

I tell of great,

very great things

to come."

DOCTOR OEDIPUS COMPLEX

Pupil of Freudanalytikus   As the narrator, rather like Cigolotti in Carlo Gozzi's *Il re cervo*, Doctor Oedipus Complex solemnly announces the "great miracles" that are about to happen in the city of Serendippo. This parody of Sigmund Freud and Carl Gustav Jung is a play on the prevailing zeitgeist and its preoccupation with the unconscious. What is Dr. Complex's brief? He is to explore the dreams and drives of human nature—perhaps even those of his own "infant soul." Freud's historic collaboration with the Burghölzli psychiatric hospital, in which Jung also had an important part to play, resonates in the words of Dr. Complex: "I must nevertheless admit that despite having long had the honor of being in the service of the great magician Freudanalytikus, I have never truly understood his high teachings."

   With his short, stocky legs, Dr. Complex presents himself to us as a solid man of his times. His slender shoulders and the nesting cones painted yellow and red that serve him as a body identify him as an intellectual rather than a man of action. His stumpy arms with sharpened tips are undoubtedly better suited to writing; after all, his strength lies in the mind. It is the mind's trains of thought that have the power to lend him wings—and that on occasion do indeed lift him up off the ground. His round head is painted black, creating a counterpart to the matte white head of Freudanalytikus. Dr. Complex's alert face and the design of his brass-plumed headdress likewise tell of the influence of his great teacher.   51

TARTAGLIA

Prime minister and Clarissa's father   Tartaglia, prime minister at the court of King Deramo, enjoys the full confidence of his sovereign—and arouses misgivings in everyone else. At times powerful, at times ridiculous, he is a bumbling schemer whose most dangerous adversary is his own tongue. Tartaglia readily resorts to blackmail and threats—only to see his authority undermined by an uncontrollable stammer. He is brimming with ambition, fury, resentment, and jealousy. "First prayers, sugar sweetness, and flattery, and then force and revenge," he muses. "And there's still arsenic, murder, and blood for all who resist me." He is desperate for his daughter Clarissa to marry the king, while his own bride will be Angela, daughter of the second minister, whether she wants it or not.

   He appears in black and red, the same red as that worn by Clarissa and the same red as adorns the throne that he is desperate for her to occupy. His magnificent mantle is indicative of his high status, while his headdress anticipates the power he aspires to. His close-set, squinting eyes tell of his myopia in both the literal and the metaphorical sense. His disproportionately long arms sway around alongside the well-fed belly that he carries proudly before him.

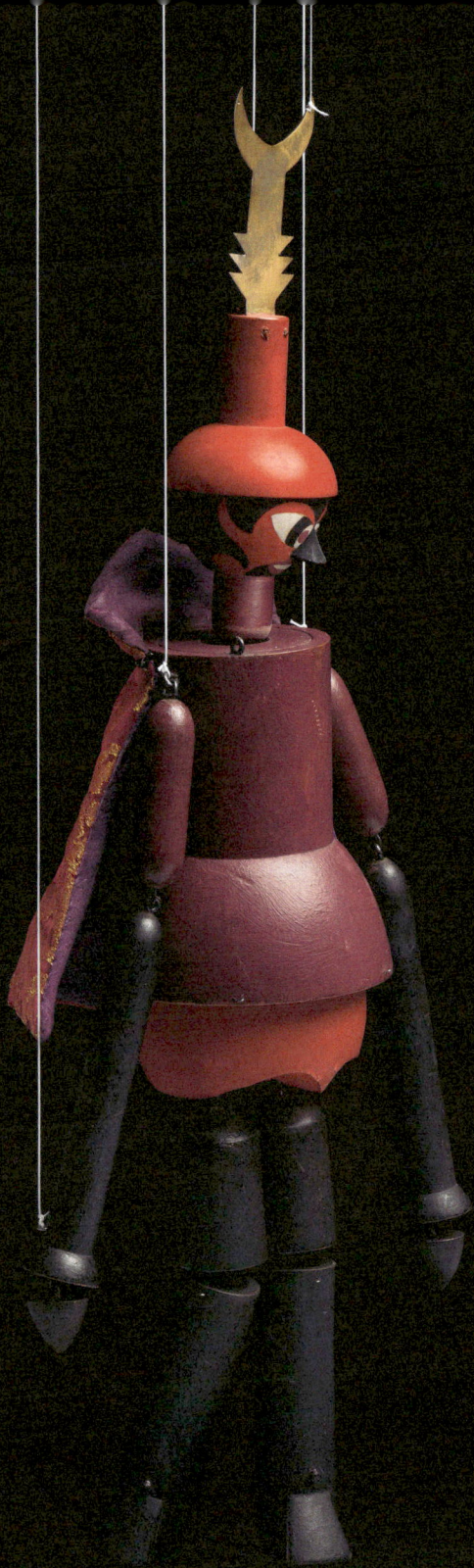

"Queen?

Me?

How that?"

Second minister and father of Angela and Leander   Pantalon, as second minister in the realm of King Deramo and father of Angela and Leander, ranks among the *vecchi*, the "elders" who in traditional commedia dell'arte play the servants' opposite numbers. Despite keeping a strict, sober watch over his family, Pantalon fails to notice that life itself has other plans in store for him. Respectable, mistrustful, and anxious to retain control, Pantalon gropes unknowingly through love's intrigues. "We know nothing," he sighs to Angela, "we know nothing." This touching ignorance makes him a tragicomic figure.

Endowed with both a moustache and beard, Pantalon matches the classical model of a commedia dell'arte *vecchio*. His advanced age is evident from his squat stature, and despite being considerably less agile than Angela and Leander, he is just as distinctive. Their cone-shaped torsos, hands, cylindrical limbs, and stylized hats identify them all as members of the same family. This likeness is further underscored by their gray and black coloration with a touch of pink. At the same time, Pantalon looks strikingly similar to the figure of Tartaglia, the play's second *vecchio*, who like him has cylindrical legs and disproportionately long forearms that seem to accentuate his stiff and awkward appearance.

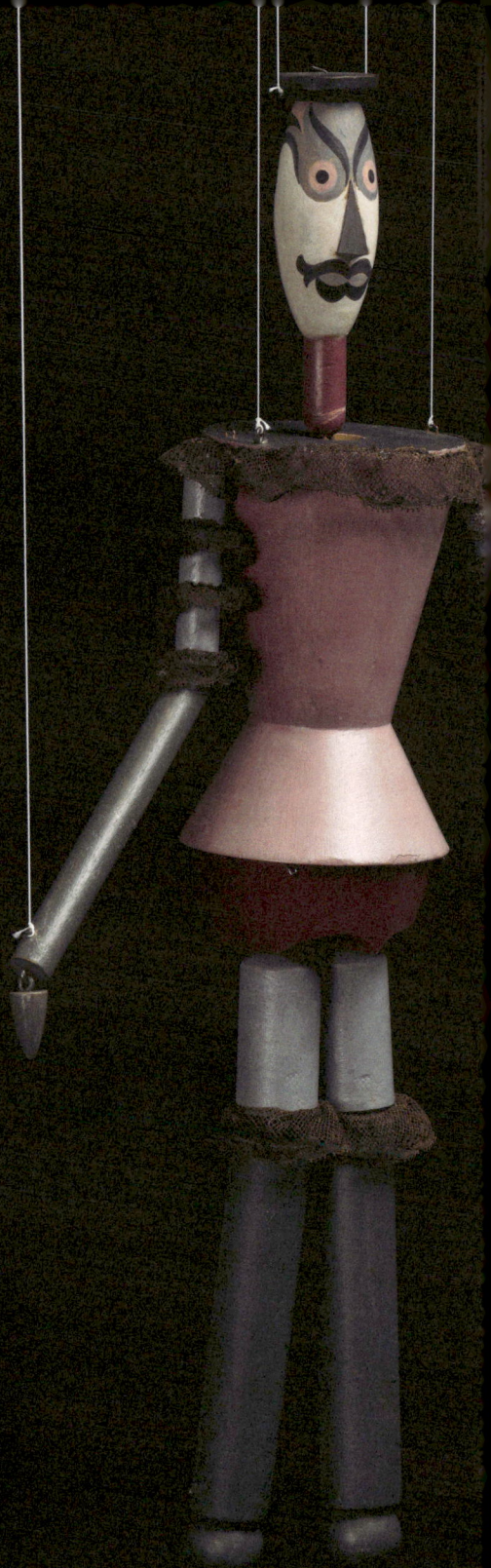

ANGELA

Daughter of the second minister Pantalon and future queen   "I am indeed so fool-ish as to be madly in love with the king!" says Angela to her father Pantalon, before offering herself to Deramo as a bride. "And if he rejects me," she sighs, "I shall surely die of it." Miserable in the belief that as she is a commoner the man she adores is unlikely to ask for her hand, she also has to fear the wrath of Tartaglia, who has been eyeing her up for himself. Tartaglia, father of her best friend Clarissa! Hence her reluctance to enter the king's secret cabinet.

Clad in a lacy dress with wide, half-length sleeves, and a high collar, Angela conveys both simple elegance and a certain down-to-earth quality—or would, were it not for the alarm signaled by the pink and white stripes on her arms and legs. She loves the king with all her heart, and has done so for a very long time. Her own actions no longer mean anything to her. Only her broad-brimmed hat seems to have a stabilizing effect. Her pale face is animated by dark strands of hair on either side and is framed at the top, as is that of her brother Leander, by arched eyebrows that make her look at once distinguished and blasé. Also clearly visible, however, are the specks of royal gold, even in her pupils. Could this be a hint that class difference will not matter so much after all, despite her father's sneer that she is a "fool" for loving the king?

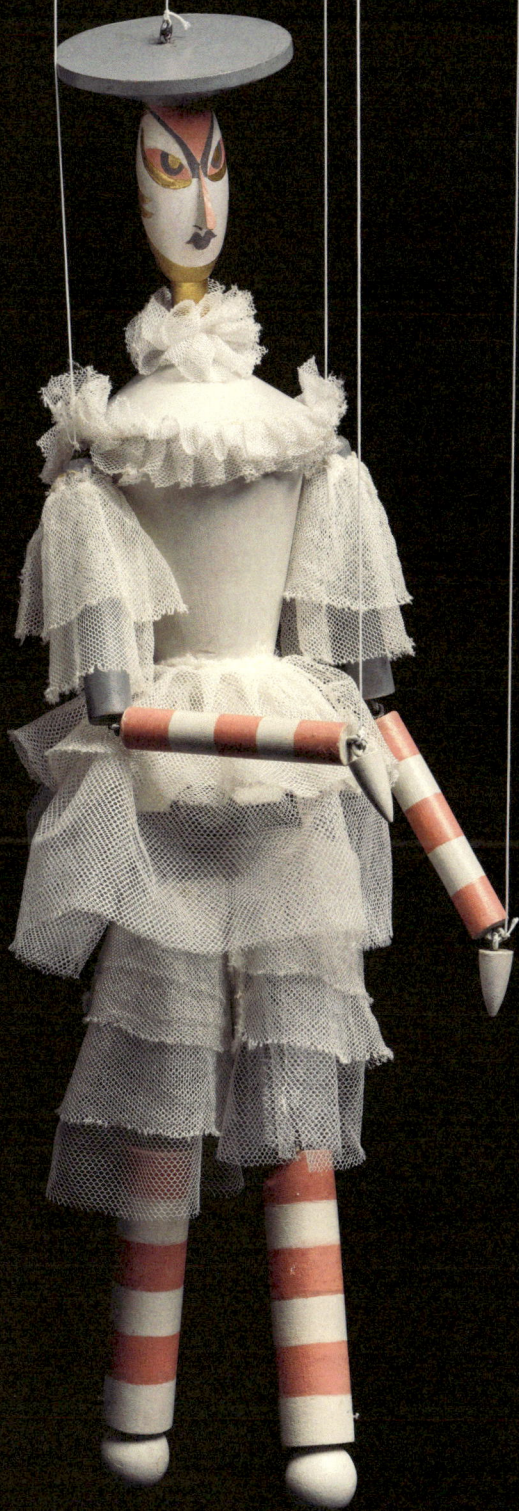

BRIGHELLA

The king's cupbearer and Smeraldina's brother   Brighella is a cunning and unscru-
pulous character, always out for his own advantage. His ambition knows no bounds:
"What bluster! My sister will ascend the throne, and whoever wishes to thwart her
will have to be more than a mangy bird. Think of our rank, of our future!" The happiness of his own sister and her sweetheart Truffaldin are of little consequence to him.
All that matters is that Smeraldina will persuade the king to love her and make her
queen, so that he, as her brother, will become "Generalissimo at the very least."
Being intellectually superior to Truffaldin, he is easily able to outwit him. He is a
clever and manipulative schemer whose eloquence and brazen impertinence consistently give him the upper hand.

    With his yellow mask-like face, his moustache, and his plain head-covering,
the figure of Brighella is clearly indebted to the model of his namesake in classical
Italian commedia dell'arte. Here, however, his cylindrical body with ogival arms
and legs marks a departure from any humanoid aspect. The rump divided into four
sections with pointed projectile limbs is mirrored by Truffaldin's feathered equiva-
lents, thus reinforcing the connection between these two servants. The bold yellows
and blues, moreover, forge a filial bond between Brighella and his flamboyantly
dressed sister Smeraldina.   74

"Oh, go to hell

and find
a husband yourself!

You're good enough
for that.

Auction yourself off,

put an advertisement

in the

Tagesanzeiger."

SMERALDINA

Brighella's sister and Truffaldin's sweetheart   Smeraldina, as the female equiva-
lent of the servants Brighella and Truffaldin, is also part of the figural repertoire of
classical commedia dell'arte. Intemperate and quick-witted, she sweeps through
the piece with a combination of charm, guile, and unbridled self-regard. She loves
Truffaldin—or has at least promised him as much—but drops him the moment a
better catch comes into view. Dressed to kill and with coquettishly fluttering eye-
lids, she unashamedly sets about seducing the king. Her ambition lends her a play-
ful levity that allows her to console Truffaldin with sweet promises even as she is
going behind his back: "To me the court, to you the forecourt!" As future queen, she
says, she will have him appointed "director of the great royal aviary."

    Her figure is a deep, radiant yellow and crowned by a feathered headdress
that she has no qualms about wearing, even though it was once a gift of Truffaldin.
Like him, she embellishes her outfit with ostentatious details, just as they both sport
the same glowing yellow as adorns Brighella. The affinity with her brother is impossible to overlook. Both figures share the same shade of bright blue, and their faces
feature a similarly impertinent nose. Smeraldina's flirtatiously raised upper lip,
moreover, is ironically echoed in Brighella's moustache.

TRUFFALDIN

Birdcatcher and Smeraldina's sweetheart   As a variation of Arlecchino, probably the commedia dell'arte's most famous figure, the birdcatcher Truffaldin has many different faces: faithful fool, cunning satirist, and jilted lover. A rogue and spinner of half-truths, his naive, absurd logic serves as a gauge of how serious and sincere the other characters' feelings are. His great love is Smeraldina. He has given her his heart—and his feathers—in exchange for a (flimsy) promise. Once ambition overtakes her, however, his affection curdles into derisory rejection: "Neither big nor little, neither cooked nor raw, neither stewed nor roasted. No, I won't. I cannot love another's leftover." Despite all setbacks, Truffaldin remains true to himself: a cheerful fellow with a critical mind, whose rather lame comparisons and ridiculous arguments provide a caustic commentary not just on the play itself but also on what was then the talk of the town in Zurich, from the ETH Zurich, whose now iconic dome had only just been finished, to the black market in saccharine that flourished during the First World War.

Clad in magnificent green and festooned with feathers, the birdcatcher is as fleet of foot as a dancer, his nose as pointed as his words. His figure is slim and articulated like that of Brighella, while his limbs double as perches for little birds that dance at his every move, as if they were an organic part of him. His face, framed by a black mask, is scored with jagged lines, and while the mouth is curled in derision, there is more than a hint of irony in his eyes.

LEANDER

Son of the second minister Pantalon and Clarissa's sweetheart   "Leander! [...] A common cavalier? You prefer Pantalon's son to the king? And you claim to be my daughter?" asks the incredulous Tartaglia of his daughter Clarissa, who is hopelessly in love with Leander, as he is with her. And here is the man himself: not a swashbuckler, but just a young man in trouble. Clarissa has been forced to present herself to King Deramo as a potential bride, and Leander is convinced that he will discover in her his "white blackbird." "I've lost Clarissa. Oh, unfortunate Leander!" he sighs.

   Leander's outfit, like that of his father, the second minister Pantalon, consists of a stylized suit with short tabs. A slim figure with long legs, he wears black, over-the-knee boots that mark him out as a nobleman. The lace trim around the top of his boots, topping the shoulders of his tunic, and encircling his upper arms underscores his high status. It also lends him a feminine touch, and a rather hesitant one at that. Leander's pale, oblong face under a flat beret derives its contours from a conspicuous moustache and beard. His bold, arched eyebrows draw attention to the eyes, which, when viewed in profile, transition seamlessly into his carefully coiffed hair. The torso is dominated by a matte red that spreads as far as the neck and that recurs in the shading of his pink eyes, reflecting Leander's state of mind. Clearly this is a figure in distress.   88

THE GUARDS

The royal palace is guarded by a cohort of sentries. They escort the marriage candidates, rally the people to rejoice at the choice of Angela, and are even on hand to throw the whole court into the dungeon. As a well-oiled, unfailingly obedient apparatus, they operate as the long arm of the law. Only in one scene do they themselves speak. On barging into Angela's bedchamber to arrest Truffaldin, they apologize to her—"Pardon me, great lady!"—while meting out much rougher treatment to Truffaldin.

In visual terms, the figure referred to as either "Guard" or "Guards" combines the aesthetic of a technical, industrially made device with formal echoes of a medieval suit of armor. The five ridged "heads" look like electrical insulators endowed with 360° vision, despite lacking the human eyes and mouth originally intended for them in the design drawings. Their individual combat-readiness concentrated in a single rump on five legs turns them into a powerful, anonymous phalanx. Their arms, moreover, bear long weapons, which when detached from the Guards serve as shotguns for the hunters. This dissociative figure paints a potent and terrifying picture of Europe as it was in 1918: that is, with war still omnipresent, dire shortages, an impending general strike, and on top of everything else, the Spanish flu.

THE STATUE

The psychoanalytical apparatus   Standing at the entrance to the king's cabinet are two statues: one of them, a gift to King Deramo from Freudanalytikus, is a magical apparatus that can unmask secret failings, duplicitous intentions, and lies, and has thus proven to be of great service to the monarch in his interrogation of potential brides. The only candidate whom the king genuinely desires is Angela, yet it is shortly before she enters that the Guards cover the two statues and exchange the figure hitherto used—a live person covered in whitewash—for a real statue made of plaster. Since this statue obviously cannot pull a face, it inevitably confirms the king's longing for true love without so much as a smirk. "Wonderful work, I thank you," cries the delighted Deramo. "When I saw that you were no longer laughing, I was gripped by fear of your magic. Whatever people say, you can still peer into their base instincts." Yet the king is mistaken, for there is no magic at work here; it is solely the stirrings of his own heart that have brought about this happy turn of events.

Primed in black with delicate white marbling, the Statue is a fine-limbed figure mounted on a solid plinth. The spindly arms and legs connected to a cone-shaped torso call to mind Javanese shadow puppets. And this figure, too, performs off in the shadows. At least visually, the Statue with neither face nor feathers stands apart from the group of figures initiated into psychoanalysis and the game of transfiguration—or would do, were it not for a tiny elbow ornament, which, given its resemblance to the hinges of the magician's spine, tells us that this miracle-working medium was a gift from Freudanalytikus.

KING DERAMO

King of the City of Serendippo and Angela's sweetheart   "It's a tough lesson, having to choose a wife," opines King Deramo, ruler of the City of Serendippo. Over the past five years, he has interrogated no fewer than 2,748 "ladies of rank" as potential wives—and has spurned them all. Only when the absence of an heir threatens to provoke social unrest and instability does he agree to also consider commoners. The king is in possession of a magic apparatus that reveals the candidates' "secret failings" so as to spare him the "indissoluble and oh so sacred bond of matrimony" with the wrong person. This gift of the scholarly Freudanalytikus turns out to be a trump card of huge importance to the state.

Painted all in gold, the figure of Deramo embodies its metaphysical meaning as symbolic of a higher power. His brocade mantle extends his stiff, upright torso, while his crown underscores his lofty elegance. Does the crown resemble antlers? And if so, does it anticipate the crucial turning point in the story? Or is it rather the kind of symmetrical blot used in a Rorschach test? It might even be said to symbolize an exceptionally intricate keyhole. Ironically, Deramo is a wreck—at least emotionally. Deep furrows line his brow, while his fragile limbs force him to proceed with caution, especially since his arms are fitted with little bells that tinkle every time he moves them. Consequently, when he finally exclaims "I have found a wife […] She is the key to my heart," we cannot help but rejoice with him. In his happiness, however, he fails to notice the malevolent machinations of his prime minister Tartaglia, who is scheming to rob him of both throne and wife.   103

THE BEAR

The forest of Roneisloppe near the Burghölzli stirs visibly as a bear suddenly crosses the path of a motley band of servile hunters: Pantalon, Leander, and Brighella. One of them clumsily shoots a "hole in the water," while another accidentally slays one of the hounds. The Bear himself remains silent. Knowing he is their prey, he nimbly outruns his pursuers and makes them look like "donkeys"—their pejorative of choice when describing themselves and each other.

The Bear, "which got away unscathed," is conceived horizontally as a four-legged puppet. His cone-shaped body widens to a flat head that ends in a blunt muzzle. As the legs differ significantly in length, the body falls away towards the forequarters, raising the rear end. Painted with a red circle outlined in pale blue, the resemblance of the Bear's backside to a target makes it irresistible to the hunters. The mask-like eyes and muzzle are painted in the same colors, which make for a bright contrast with the conspicuously matte brown of the fur. The roughly torn adhesive strips approximating a face were added at a later date. After all, as a potential hunting trophy, the Bear would not have had anything to smile about.

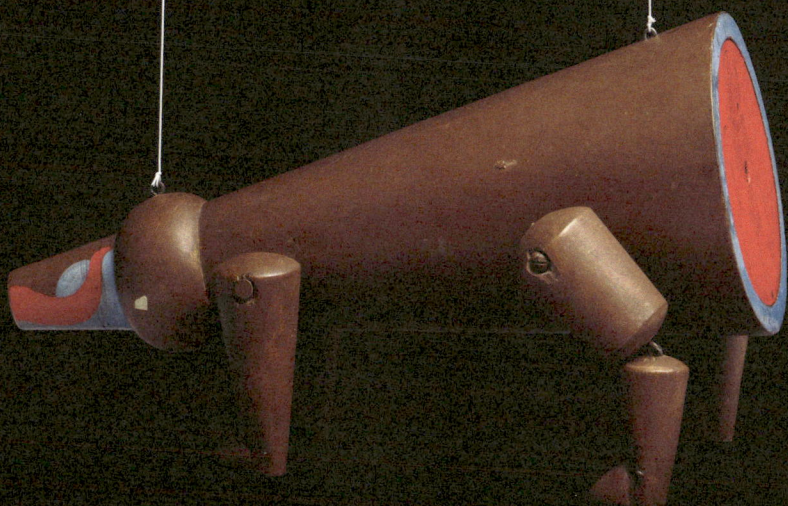

"I must return
to my castle

and my
precious wife

this

very evening."

THE PARROT

A metamorphosis of Freudanalytikus   Just as in Carlo Gozzi's play, *Il re* cervo, so in *King Stag*: a wonder-working parrot turns up to the premiere performance, proving that there is more to the "potent mysteries" of Freudanalytikus than the purple prose of the prologue spoken by Doctor Complex. Indeed, the final act sees the great magician invoking the power of the Urlibido and voluntarily regressing into a parrot; and while propriety does not allow the Parrot's role as a Jungian symbol of the libido to be spelled out in front of the ladies in the audience, Freudanalytikus himself, in his avian incarnation, freely admits that "centuries-old things take on an exotic hue in my beak: old meaning and new blather, an old, but eternally new truth."
    With his pale blue feet, the Parrot seems better suited to decorative standing than flight. Colored "white and red after the latest fashion," he stands out from the rest of the ensemble. Only a little stylized in appearance, his movable head can turn freely in all directions, allowing the pattern of circle segments, born of the creator's concrete language of forms and painted onto it, to be studied. As a parrot, Freudanalytikus becomes extremely loquacious and persuades even Truffaldin to take action. While the birdcatcher sports plenty of real feathers, the Parrot has only a single, sheet-metal tail feather, presumably to signal the affinity with Freudanalytikus's head ornament.

"Fall away, feathers!"

FREUDANALYTIKUS

King Deramo's analyst   Like his famous namesake Freud, Freudanalytikus, the "great magician, astronomer, physician, and physicist" leaves Vienna to pay his second visit to Serendippo (Zurich) in 1918, five years after the first. It was then that he first psychoanulyzed King Deramo himself, and in the process shared "two potent mysteries" with him. After some turbulent scenes and a dramatic quest for power, wealth, and recognition, Freudanalytikus turns to face the audience to deliver his concluding soliloquy, in which he proclaims the benefits of his theory: "You have seen the wonders of my powers. Urlibido, the salt in every sap, soon turns man into beast. [...] and it is my wisdom's most sacred duty to find you in every form and in every person."

His eccentrically positioned legs under an elongated torso make the magician's gait a balancing act. The convex disks connecting his "vertebrae" seem to amplify that basic instability, while his long arms remain adept at pulling the levers of power. There are echoes of the "blue magic" practiced by the magician in the coloration of both his shrewd eyes and sagacious lips. In terms of design, the figure is closely related to Dr. Complex in that his ovoid head is encased in a pink cap topped with a stylized brass plume. The black sidelocks peeping out from under it are of a piece with his fetching goatee beard.

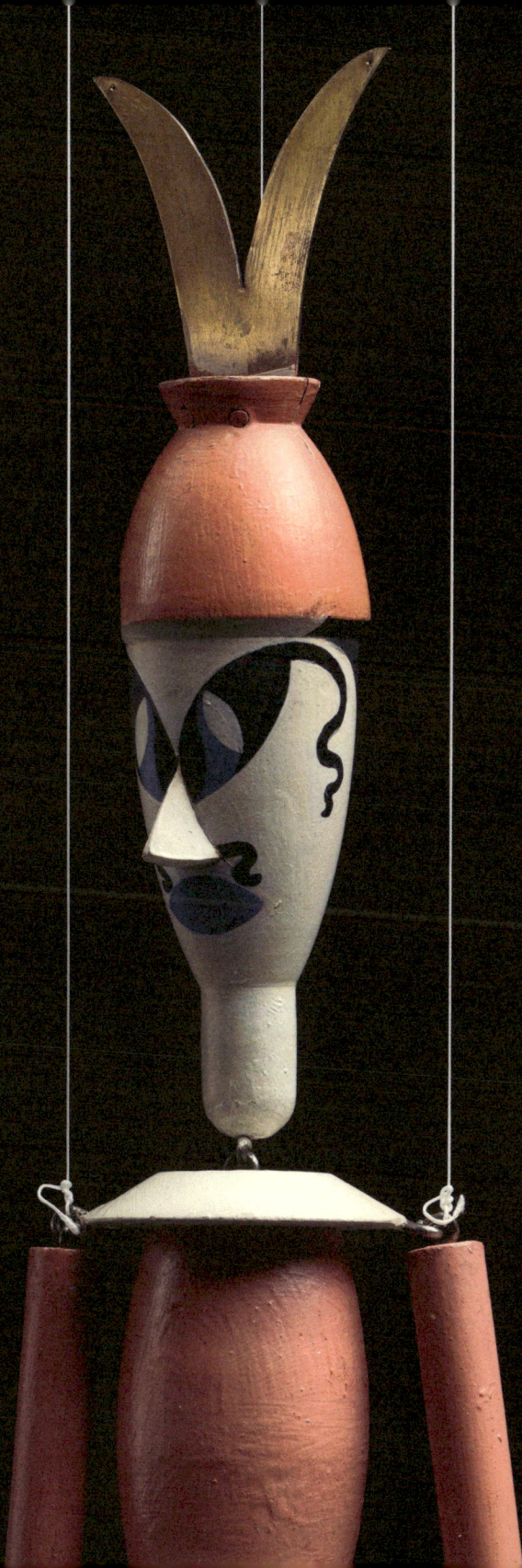

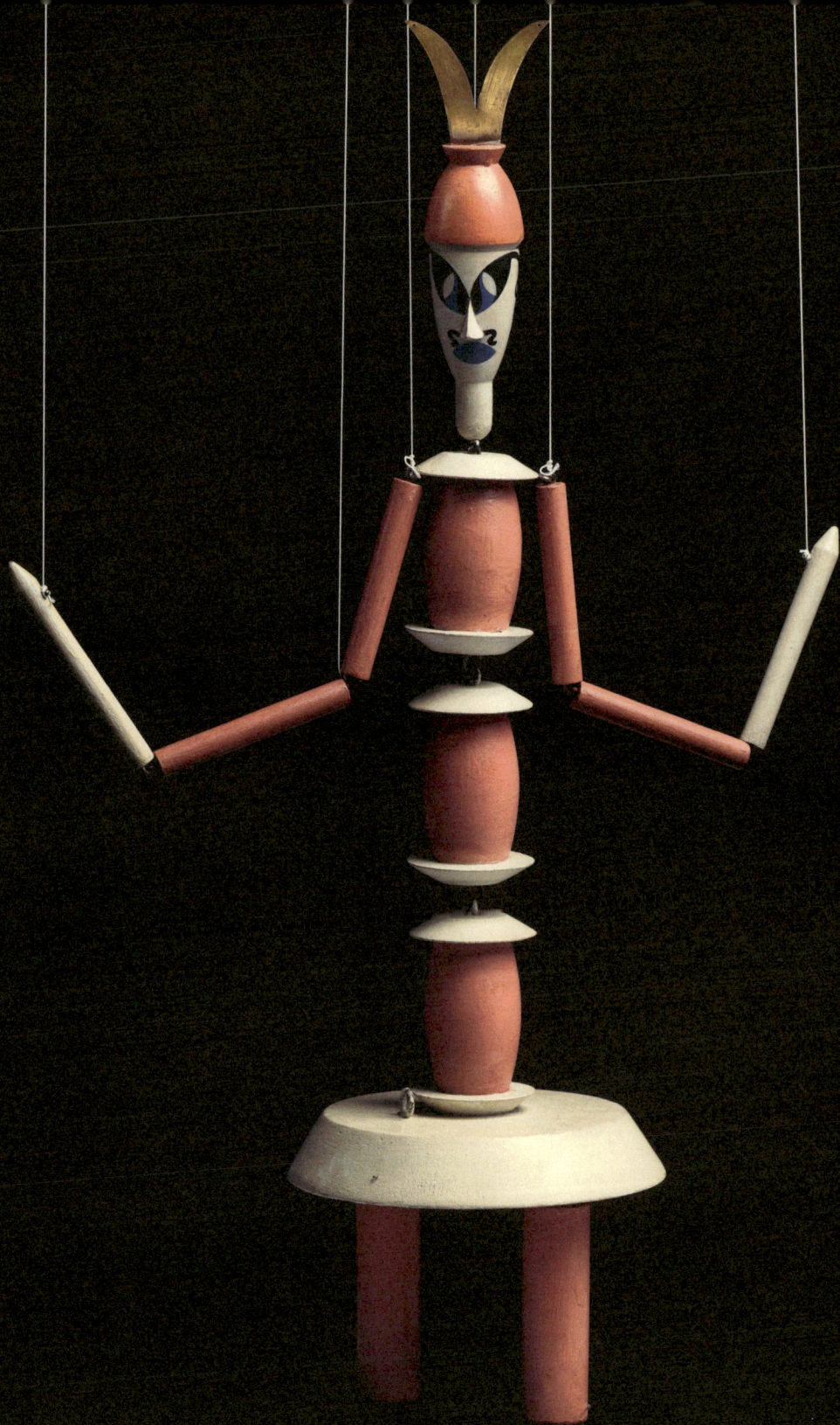

"Only he
who analyzes his soul

and smooths out

every fold in it

with the power
of our wise
wonderworks—

only he can hope

to match

me."

THE SCRIPT

König Hirsch

Carlo Gozzi, *König Hirsch (King Stag)*, revised by
René Morax, translated and expanded by Werner Wolff,
typescript, Act 1, Scene 3, 33.1 × 22.1 cm, 1918

3. Szene.

Pantalon und Angela.

Pantalon: Man weiss nichts, meine liebe Tochter, man weiss
nichts. 2748 Prinzessinnen und hohe Frauen sind vom König ver-
schmäht worden. Jch führe sie in eines geheimes Kabinett, dort
stellt er jhnen drei oder vier Fragen und dann schickt er sie
mit Höflichkeit nach Hause. Es gefällt ihm Stimme nicht oder Ihr
Witz gefällt ihm nicht oder dann hat er solch ein feines Unter-
scheidungsvermögen, dass er irgend eine kleine Affäre im Jnnern
entdeckt, die ihm nicht zusagt oder vielleicht hat er irgend
einen kleinen Fehler gesehen. Man weiss es nicht. Er ist nicht
überspannt; denn seit ich ihm diene, habe ich oft erfahren, dass
er ein vernünftiger Mann ist, zuvorkommend und mit allen Talen-
ten, die ein Monarch haben kann, begabt. Aber hinter dieser Geschichte steckt der Teufel, das ist sicher wahr.

Angela: Lieber Vater, warum hast Du Dich nicht widersetzt, mich
einer so grossen Schande auszusetzen? Wenn er mich abweist und
so wird es kommen, müsste ich vor Betrübnis sterben.

Pantalon: Oh, er wird Dich sicherlich abweisen. Jch habe mich
auf die Knie geworfen und gebeten, Dir zu erlassen, mit den an-
dern zu erscheinen. Jch habe ihm gesagt, dass wir als Bürger von
Venedig geboren sind, dass wir arme aber ehrenwerte Leute sind
und nur durch seine Grossmut erhöht wurden, dass wir nicht wert
sind, an einer solch grossen Ehre teil zu haben. Nichts hat ge-
nützt. Er hat Dich in die Urne geworfen, Du bist als dritte
herausgekommen. Was bleibt da zu sagen? Wir müssen hingehen.

Angela: So viel Nichtigkeit vor so viel Grösse, das macht mich
zittern. Doch wenn er bei seiner Prüfung aufrichtig und mit
Wahrhaftigkeit die Liebe sucht....

Pantalon: Bist Du verliebt, Närrin?

6

123

Carlo Gozzi, *König Hirsch (King Stag)*, revised by
René Morax, translated and expanded by Werner Wolff,
typescript, Act 1, Scene 5, 33.1 × 22.1 cm, 1918

Truffaldin:-platzt vor Lachen-: Oh-oh-oh! Ah-ah-ah!
Smeraldina! Ah-ah-ah! Die Königin von Saba.

Smeraldina: Jch bin es, Truffaldin, ich, Smeraldina.

Truffaldin: Du, mein Täubchen, mit diesem Feuerwerk auf dem
Kopf und diesem Fliegenfänger, diesem Rosenstrauch. Gehst Du
auf den Karneval, oder willst Du Dich aufs Spalier setzen, die
Spatzen zu verscheuchen? Oh-oh-oh!   -er lacht-

Brighella: Höre, mein lieber Truffaldin, die edle Smeraldina,
meine Schwester, wird an dem Wettstreit beim König teil nehmen.

Truffaldin: Sie, an dem Wettstreit beim König? Nein, nein, an
der Konkurrenz für Vogelscheuchen! Dort wird sie den ersten
Preis bekommen.

Smeraldina:Still, Hanswurst. Eine Dame von meiner Zukunft, von
meiner Taille und meinem Rang erduldet es nicht, derart belei-
digt zu werden. Komm, mein Bruder!

Truffaldin: Jst es also wahr? Jhr geht ins schwarze Kabinett ?

Smeraldina: -macht eine Reverenz-: So ists, so ists, mein Herr.

Brighella: Wir verlieren unsere Zeit mit einem Tölpel. Nimm
meinen Arm und lass uns zum König gehen
-Sie wollen hinaus gehen, Truffaldin verhindert sie daran.-

Truffaldin: Nur mit meiner Erlaubnis, Madame. Erinnere Dich,
Smeraldina, erinnere Dich an das Wort, das Du mir gestern Abend
gegeben hast, als ich Deinen Strumpf mit einem grünen Seiden-
band aufgebunden. Jch habe Dir einen Ring, der fast aus Gold ist,
gegeben, diese Pfauenfeder auf Deinem Kopf, einen Kamm, der noch
alle seine Zähne hat wie ich, und ein Stück Wachs für Deinen
Faden. Und Du, Du gabst mir Dein Wort. Hier liegt es auf meinem
Herzen.

9

124

Jch lasse Dich nicht ins königliche Kabinett, ich lasse Dich nicht, Verräterin.

Smeraldina: Vor des Königs Befehl sind alle Schwüre Papierfetzen.

Truffaldin: Jch sage alles dem König, alles.

Brighella: Possen, Possen! Meine Schwester wird den Thron besteigen, und das darf kein kümmerlicher Vogel sein, der sie daran hindern will. Denke an unsern Rang, an unsere Zukunft!

Truffaldin: So willst Du mich verraten? Oh Schmerz, oh Trauer, oh meine vielgeliebte Smeraldina, Du grausame!

Smeraldina: Weine nicht, Truffaldin. Du musst auf der Höhe der Begebenheiten bleiben. Wenn ich morgen Königin von Serendippo bin, so wird Deine Königin nicht undankbar sein. Du wirst 1000 Goldzechinen mit meinem Bildnis bekommen und die Stelle des Direktors des grossen königlichen Vogelbauers, ~~Mir der Hof, Dir der Vorhof!~~ Du wirst meinen Kanarienvögeln das Singen lehren.

Brighella: Komm, Schwester. Wir dürfen den König nicht warten lassen.
        -Er gibt ihr den Arm und geht mit ihr majestätisch ab.
        Truffaldin weint. Leander tritt ein.-

                        6. Szene.

                Leander, Truffaldin.

Truffaldin: (weint-): Ach Gott!

Leander: Ach Gott!

Truffaldin: O Smeraldina!

The title of the original script of Act 1 of *King Stag* is handwritten in pen and ink on a finely drawn pencil line in the top right-hand corner of the cover. The flimsy sheets of parchment paper are bound in brown paper and the bundle is held together by a narrow cloth spine. Frequent use has left the pages slightly crumpled and brittle. Besides being in possession of two editions of this handy booklet of Act 1, the Museum für Gestaltung Zürich holds individually bound scripts for Acts 2 and 3 as well as both acts together in a single volume, albeit in a different format (paper formats having yet to be standardized). Presumably the scripts belonged to the speakers of the various parts, which would explain the handwritten directions on vocal pitch and how the marionettes should stand or move. Occasionally, there are suggestions for a reordering of the syntax or minor additions to the text.

The program of the first performance of *King Stag* names the author of the play as "Gozzi," referring to the Venetian playwright Carlo Gozzi, whose 1762 stage play *Il re cervo* combined typical commedia dell'arte tropes with fairy-tale elements. With the Swiss Werkbund's large exhibition on the horizon in 1918, the Werkbund committee responsible for the Schweizerisches Marionettentheater (Swiss Puppet Theater) commissioned the dramatists René Morax and Werner Wolff with a contemporary reworking of the piece by Gozzi. Both had puppet plays of their own on the exhibition program: *La machine volante* and *Le Baladin de satin cramoisi* by Morax, and *Der Mann aus einer anderen Welt* and *Die beiden Brüder* by Wolff, in French and German respectively.

For *King Stag*, the playwrights decided to forgo the different idioms on which much of the entertainment value of the Italian original rested, and opted instead for local references and acerbic wit to keep the audience amused, as when Truffaldin introduces the Parrot as follows: "Your Majesty will see that he has a voice as mellifluous as a priest. He is quite the cosmopolitan and speaks more languages than a hotel doorman: Italian, Russian, German, English, Dutch, French, American, Spanish, Chinese, Zurich dialect, and hence also Dada."

The English version of the text is based on the German transcription, with the aim of remaining as close as possible to the original script. For the sake of readability, however, formal aspects of the text—for example, the stage directions—have nevertheless been standardized. Scene 6, which was inadvertently assigned twice in Act 3, is indicated as Scene 6 [1] and 6 [2].

KING STAG

Act 1

Scene 1: Prologue

The prologue is spoken by Doctor Complex,
a very serious-looking gentleman
with gold-rimmed glasses, a frock coat,
and a large book tucked under his arm.
He greets the audience and declaims solemnly,
as if preaching from a pulpit.

Doctor Complex: Ladies and gentlemen, honored guests, I tell
of great, very great things to come. Five years have passed
since a great magician, astronomer, physician, and physicist,
a man in possession of white magic, black magic, green magic,
and, I believe, even blue magic, came to our city of Serendippo. He called himself the great Freudanalytikus, and I am
his lowly and loyal pupil, Dr. Oedipus Complex. No sooner
had Deramo, king of this city, learned that my master, Freudanalytikus, had taken a room at the Hotel Bellevue, than
he called for his trusty prime minister and said to him:
Tartaglia—that being the name of that most worthy minister—
my dear Tartaglia, go to the Bellevue Palace and escort
the magician Freudanalytikus back to the Royal Palace. And so
it came to pass.—To describe the splendor of the welcome
accorded my master would be too tedious. Suffice it to say
that, on his departure for Vienna, he left our majesty with
two great testimonies of his regard: two potent magical
mysteries, two biological wonders, two symbolic natural phe-
nomena. These I cannot reveal to you now, as you are to
have the pleasure of seeing them for yourselves. I must nevertheless admit that despite having long had the honor of
being in the service of the great magician Freudanalytikus,

I have never truly understood his high teachings. But he did once say to me: My son, beware! Never to speak to anyone of the secrets that I entrusted to the King of Serendippo in the year 1913. Explore the dreams and the drives of human nature; dive down into your innermost self and bring to light the polymorphous sexuality of your infant soul. Fathom your own heart, fathom, above all, the heart of women. But then, in 1918, on the 18th day of the month of May, you shall carry me in the form of a parrot into the forest of Roneisloppe near the Burghölzli—and there abandon me. Great miracles will arise out of those two mysteries, for know this, my dear Oedipus Complex, through Urlibido, the queen of all souls, I have been degraded to the condition of parrots. Be sure not to forget to carry me into the Burghölzli forest in the year 1918, for it is from there that a birdcatcher shall take me away, and I shall let two great miracles happen. See, that is the power of Urlibido!—On saying this, Freudanalytikus shed his human form and became a magnificent parrot.

The meaning of a parrot in the key to all dreams is something you gentlemen scarcely need me to explain, and you ladies even less so. But let us not speak of that! For those who are not yet initiated into our mysteries of nature would soon enough slander us. Besides, there are young ladies present. And they will see quite different things here, namely King Deramo's magic cabinet with its magical apparatus for psychoanalyzing women. So now I shall leave to take the magic parrot into the forest near the Burghölzli, and you shall see exactly what you shall see. Meanwhile, I wish you health, patience, perseverance, and attentiveness, good digestion, and—should our poetic arts bore you—sound sleep, and a pleasant journey back to childhood or, to use the correct term for it, regression into infantilism.

Scene 2

A room in the palace.
Tartaglia and Clarissa.

Tartaglia: (stuttering here and there) Clarissa, my daughter, have we not had great good fortune here in the Kingdom of Serendippo? You became a lady here, and I prime minister, feared by all and much loved by our King Deramo. Today, the moment has come for us to take a great leap, dear Clarissa, and if you obey me, you shall be crowned queen before the day is out.

Clarissa: Queen? Me? How that?

Tartaglia: Yes, queen! ... Queen! For you know very well that our King Deramo, having interrogated 2,748 maidens, princesses, and other ladies of rank in his secret cabinet and found them all wanting—damned if I know why!—resolved four years ago never to marry.

Clarissa: Yes, I know. And you believe that after rejecting so many high-ranking ladies, he would want to make me his wife?

Tartaglia: (aloud) Silly girl! If I say so, you can be sure that I know what I'm talking about. Just yesterday, I cleverly dissuaded him by pointing out that the throne has no heir, that there is widespread discontent, and that, incited by foreign agitators, the people are beginning to revolt, the deserters are striking and so on and so forth, so that finally, I was able to convince him that at last the time had come for him to take a wife. But he is still obsessed with this accursed idea of first interrogating such a maiden in his secret cabinet. And since there are no more princesses to be

3

thus scrutinized, he has decided to announce that now any mademoiselle at all, no matter what her station or place of origin might be, may now seek admission to that damned secret cabinet. The names of two hundred maidens have already been gathered and lots have been drawn to determine the order in which they are to be presented. Your name, Clarissa, was the first to be drawn and you must now make yourself ready for your hearing. He is only doing right by me, for you are my daughter and he is no man-eater. If you conduct yourself well, I am certain that you shall become queen before the day is out and I the most brilliant man on earth. (quietly) Tell me, dear daughter, I hope you don't have any hidden blemishes that he may yet discover? What what?

Clarissa: Oh, dear father, give me but this, spare me this trial, I beg you!

Tartaglia: What? What's this? Silly goose! You shall present yourself to the king forthwith and shall pass the test! Otherwise... have I made myself clear... You know me.... Are you going to obey me, Miss Snotty-Nose? (softly) Is it some secret flaw of yours, or what is it?

Clarissa: I have none. But I'm so ashamed. I shall not perform well at this trial; it is impossible! I shall be rejected!

Tartaglia: No talk of shame! No talk of rejection! There'll be none of that. Off we go! It's time. He's waiting for you in his cabinet. (takes her by the arm)

Clarissa: (reluctantly) No, father, no.

Tartaglia: I'll rip your ears off! I'm telling you to come and to pass this test with flying colors! If not... (applying force)

4

Clarissa: But father, I cannot. I'll never pass the test.
I love Leander and will love him to the day I die. I would
never be strong enough to hide my love from the king.

Tartaglia: (furiously steps back) Leander! You mean Pantalon
the second minister's son? A common cavalier? You prefer
Pantalon's son to the king? And you claim to be my daughter?
What a pitiful, unworthy daughter of the great Tartaglia!
Have I made myself clear? If you discover this demeaning love
of yours to the king, if you cannot declare him to be your
choice... Have I made myself clear? Let us go! Not another
word! (takes her by the arm)

Clarissa: Have mercy on me and spare me that! I have no wish
to hurt my friend Angela by becoming her rival, for I know of
her undying love for the king.

Tartaglia: (turns back) Angela, Pantalon's daughter, loves
the king! (to himself) Angela, my own heart's desire, whom I
intended to marry today, with or without her consent! She
loves the king? (aloud) Clarissa, listen to me and tremble!
If you do not present yourself to the king forthwith, if
you reveal to him your love for Leander, if you do not persuade him to choose you as his wife, and if you elect not to
care about my conversation with the king, the poison is
waiting. Death is ready for you.

Clarissa: (horrified) I shall obey. You shall be satisfied.
You shall see me rejected and dishonored.

Tartaglia: (drags her away) No more dithering! Think of your
life, of my command, you stupid, imbecilic, silly, snotty-
nosed child. (exuent)

Scene 3

Pantalon and Angela.

Pantalon: We know nothing, my dear daughter, we know nothing. The king has already spurned 2,748 princesses and ladies of rank. I take them to a secret cabinet, where he asks them three or four questions, and then politely sends them home again. He may not like her voice or wit, or he has powers of discernment so fine that he is able to discover in them some minor matter that he likes not, or sees some fault in them. We do not know. He is not overwrought; for as long as I have been serving him, I have often seen him to be a reasonable man, both courteous and amply endowed with all the talents that a monarch can have. Yet behind this story lurks the devil—that much is certain.

Angela: But father, dear, why did you not resist exposing me to such shame? If he rejects me, which is what will happen, the grief is sure to kill me.

Pantalon: Of course he will reject you. I went on my knees before him to beg that you be spared having to appear before him with the others. I told him that we were born citizens of Venice, that we are poor but honorable people who have been raised up only through his magnanimity, that we are not worthy to partake of such a great honor. But it was all to no avail. He threw your name into the urn and it was the third to be drawn. What more can I say? We have to go there.

Angela: The idea of such a nobody before such greatness makes me tremble. But if, by means of this test, he is truly and sincerely seeking love....

Pantalon: You're not in love, are you, you fool?

Angela: Knowing you love me, dear father, I can confess to you that I am. I am indeed so foolish as to be madly in love with the king! And if he rejects me, I shall surely die of it.

Pantalon: Oh no! And I, poor man, understand you!

Angela: And what I fear most about this is the hostility of Tartaglia. He is very ambitious for his daughter and looks at me like one besotted, sighing all the while, and this morning he persuaded me to pretend sickness that I might not have to appear in the king's cabinet.

Pantalon: Well, that's just splendid! Another romance! God bless you for it! This is all too much!—It's getting late and we have to go. You are the third.

Angela: I shall entrust myself to the God of Love, who else? (exuent)

Scene 4

Brighella and Smeraldina.
Both in oriental garb,
Smeraldina with a huge fan,
huge flowers, and a plume.

Brighella: Now, keep your head straight and stop contorting your arms like the devil himself. Just an hour ago I was giving you lessons and testing you, but all for nothing. You remind me of one of those girls who cry out: Fresh roses! Sugared olives!

7

Smeraldina: What, little brother? Do you not believe that I was created to make even an animal fall in love with me? And how much more a king?

Brighella: What a way to speak! If you express such feelings in front of his majesty, you'll have to learn to love having your ears boxed too! I'd far rather have seen you as a spruce Venetian with a fine veil and a casually tossed-back cape.

Smeraldina: Oh, you fool! If I went to Venice dressed like this, I bet you I'd make all Venetians of good taste fall in love with me, and that the city's seamstresses would all get busy creating ten new fashions modeled on my apparel.

Brighella: Undoubtedly! All things new are pleasing, and if you had introduced yourself to the King of Serendippo as a Venetian, you would also have stood out as new. Our business is far from being on the right track. You know, if you can only make the king love you, you will become queen, and I, your brother, Generalissimo at the very least.

Smeraldina: Oh, if all I have to do is make him fall in love with me, then let me get down to it. I've prepared the world's most beautiful sighs, the most seductive swoons. I can easily sing the enchanting verses of Ariosto: (sings as if at the opera) Che per amor venne in forore [sic], e matto L'nom [sic], che si saggio era stimato prima.

Brighella: Enough! What caterwauling! And the figure you cut! ... Worse still! Off we go, let's throw ourselves into the sea! (They are about to leave when Truffaldino [sic] enters.)

As before with Truffaldin. Truffaldin is
dressed in oriental garb, green like a birdcatcher
but with a comically laced-up bodice.

Truffaldin: (bursts out laughing) Oh-oh-oh! Ah-ah-ah!
Smeraldina! Ah-ah-ah! The Queen of Sheba.

Smeraldina: It's me, Truffaldin—me, Smeraldina.

Truffaldin: You, my little dove? With that firework on your
head, that flycatcher, that bunch of roses? Are you off to
carnival, or are you going to perch on top of the trellis to
scare away the sparrows? Oh-oh-oh! (laughs)

Brighella: Listen, dear Truffaldin, the noble Smeraldina, my
sister, is to take part in the contest before the king.

Truffaldin: Her, in a contest before the king? Surely not!
More like a contest for scarecrows, where she would be sure
to win first prize.

Smeraldina: Be quiet, you clown! A lady of my prospects, my
rank, my waistline, will not suffer being offended in such a
way. Come, brother!

Truffaldin: So it's true? You're going to enter the black
cabinet?

Smeraldina: (curtsies) So it is, so it is, my lord.

Brighella: We're wasting our time with this booby. Take my
arm and let us proceed to the king. (They are about to leave
when Truffaldin blocks their way.)

<u>Truffaldin</u>: Only with my permission, Madame. Do you remember, Smeraldina, how yesterday evening, while I was tying your stockings with a green silk ribbon, you gave me your word? And how I gave you a ring as good as gold, this peacock's plume on your head, a comb that still has all its teeth, just like me, and a piece of wax for your thread? And how you gave me your word, your word that is now pressed against my heart. I shall not let you go to the king's cabinet! I shall not let you, traitor!

<u>Smeraldina</u>: Vows are but scraps of paper compared to the king's command.

<u>Truffaldin</u>: I shall tell the king everything, everything.

<u>Brighella</u>: What bluster! My sister will ascend the throne, and whoever wishes to thwart her will have to be more than a mangy bird. Think of our rank, of our future!

<u>Truffaldin</u>: So you're going to betray me? What agony! What grief! Oh, my beloved Smeraldina, you are so cruel!

<u>Smeraldina</u>: Do not weep, Truffaldin. You must move with the times. If, tomorrow, I am Queen of Serendippo, your queen will not be ungrateful. You shall receive a thousand gold pieces with my likeness on them and shall be appointed direc-tor of the great royal aviary. To me the court, to you the forecourt! You shall teach my canaries to sing.

<u>Brighella</u>: Come now, sister. We must not keep the king waiting. (He gives her his arm and they exit majestically. Truffaldin weeps. Enter Leander)

10

Scene 6

Leander, Truffaldin.

Truffaldin: (weeping) Oh god!

Leander: Oh god!

Truffaldin: Oh, Smeraldina!

Leander: Oh, Clarissa!

Truffaldin: Smeraldina, Queen of Serendippo! Oh!

Leander: Clarissa, Deramo's wife! Oh!

Truffaldin: She's so beautiful, so strong, so solid!

Leander: She's so delicate, so gentle, so fine!

Truffaldin: Her brother, that ruffian Brighella, is to blame.
He'd sell even their own mother and grandmother.

Leander: Her father Tartaglia is the ambitious one driving
her into the king's arms, whereas I am the one she loves.

Truffaldin: I adore her!

Leander: Yet who would be worthier of becoming queen
than Clarissa?

Truffaldin: Smeraldina! I tell you, Mr. Leander, my beloved
is the one who will be chosen.

11

Leander: And I tell you, donkey, that Clarissa is the one who will become queen. 2,748 maidens have already submitted to the king's scrutiny and he still hasn't found his white blackbird!

Truffaldin: No, Smeraldina outshines them all, as the moon outshines the stars or the pumpkin outshines the beans. That skin, that healthy bloom, those cheeks like tomatoes, that bosom! God in heaven, that bosom with those two hemispheres, that map of the world!

Leander: I've lost Clarissa. Oh, unfortunate Leander! (exits, weeping)

Truffaldin: Smeraldina is lost! If King Deramo rejects her—ha ha!—then doubtless he will have his reasons. And I have no appetite for what others deride. So what else is left?..... She is lost. (exits)

Scene 7

Change of scene to the cabinet of King Deramo,
the door to which is in the middle.
On either side of the door are niches
containing statues.
The statue on the left is a living person,
visible down to the knees and white
so that the viewer might mistake him
for a plaster cast like the one on the right.
Presumably this statue is one
of the great mysteries that the magician
Freudanalytikus gifted King Deramo,
as promised in the Prologue.
In the middle of the cabinet are two cushions
on which to recline, following
the oriental custom.

Deramo: (alone) It's a tough lesson, having to choose a wife.
(turning to the bust) I am following you, Freudanalytikus!
Your gift here, this bust, will laugh at even the whitest of
lies told by these mendacious ladies. By faithfully uncover-
ing their secret failings, it has so far spared me that
indissoluble and oh so sacred bond of matrimony. Oh, analyzer
of souls, wondrous mystery: Do not abandon me today! And
every time a maiden full of faults and lies presents herself
to me today, give me a sign by laughing at her deceit. Here
comes Tartaglia's daughter. Let's see whether she is honest.
After all that I have experienced, it seems to me all but
impossible that a woman might tell the truth.

Scene 8

Clarissa and Deramo; Guards
accompanying Clarissa. Clarissa enters
through the door in the middle.
The Guards who precede her, and will
shortly let her pass, cover up the busts.
At a sign from the king, they leave
the cabinet and lock the door.

Deramo: Sit down, Clarissa! My presence should not arouse so
much as an iota of fear in you. Answer my free questions
freely.

Clarissa: (sadly) My lord and king, what magnanimity! Since I
must obey, I shall indeed sit down. (sits)

Deramo: Today I must find a consort for myself, and you are
probably the one most worthy of me. Would not the daughter of
Tartaglia, who after all is dear to me, be worthy of my
hand? Yet I would first like to hear it from your lips that
you will gladly accept this hand.

Clarissa: Who could be displeased by an offer of marriage
to such a great king, a king so illustrious, so noble, such a
paragon of faith and virtue?

Deramo: (turning, unnoticed by Clarissa, to the Statue, from
which no sign is forthcoming) That, in a nutshell, is the
answer. But I want to hear it from you. I know very well that
such a marriage would be a most attractive prospect for many,
many ladies, though perhaps Clarissa does not number herself
among that great throng? I have asked you a question and I
want to know your answer.

Clarissa: (to herself) Oh, heavens! What compulsion! [(to Deramo)] How could you believe, my lord, that I alone would be so proud as to embrace such happiness begrudgingly?

Deramo: (turning to the Statue) Clarissa, your words are not clear. I beg you, I want to know it from you alone: This marriage, tell me, is it what you wish? I am speaking of you!

Clarissa: (to herself) It is you, cruel father, who has forced me to lie like this. [(to Deramo)] Yes, my king, whom I love, it is what I wish.

Deramo: (turning to the Statue, which laughs and then freezes again) Clarissa, I know that you are perhaps fearful of saying "It pleases me not," doubtless because you are afraid of hurting me. Might not your heart already belong to another, whom you love?

Clarissa: (to herself) I am lying only for you, cruel father. [(to Deramo)] No, great lord, my king. It is to you alone that I owe love.

Deramo: (turning to the Statue, which again laughs and then stops laughing) Well, Clarissa, go! Now I know all. I shall put the others to the test and draw my own conclusions.

Clarissa: (rises and bows) May heaven make him despise me that I might remain with Leander! (The Guard steps inside and covers the bust. Clarissa leaves, followed by the Guard.)

15

Scene 9

Deramo alone.

Deramo: How strange! I believed I'd already found an honest
girl. (to the Statue) Wonderful work, I thank you. When
I saw that you were no longer laughing, I was gripped by fear
of your magic. Whatever people say, you can still peer into
their base instincts. They may act a part, tell tall tales,
and boast, and you just smile your gentle smile, Freudanalytikus, smiling on that primal power with that first and last
smile of our innermost souls.

Scene 10

Smeraldina, Guards, and Deramo.
The Guards as above. Smeraldina approaches with
ridiculously over-the-top bowing and scraping.

Deramo: Who are you? Sit down! (to himself) Truly, it seems
to me this is the cupbearer's sister.

Smeraldina: It is I, your grace, I, sister of Brighella of
Lombardy, from an ancient noble line. While a dire misfortune
did indeed bring us low, now this way, now that, never did
poverty corrupt my proud blood.

Deramo: (turning to the Statue, which is laughing) Good, now
tell me, Lady of Lombardy, do you love me?

Smeraldina: (sighs heavily) Tyrant! What a question?!
You compelled me... Ah.. oh... hi... oh... ah!

Deramo: (looking at the Statue, which is still laughing) Were
I to choose you to be my wife and were I then to die
before you, tell me, would you take pleasure in your life as
a widow?

Smeraldina: (gesturing comically) What horrible thing is
that? Are you a tiger? Alone the thought of it, such pain..
it is too much to bear.... (She feigns a swoon.)

Deramo: (looking at the Statue, which is laughing heartily)
I'm not having much luck here. I'll summon the men to take
this Lady of Lombardy away.

Smeraldina: (hears voices and comes round)

Deramo: Madame, your love is too great. So great it makes me
afraid. Are you already a widow or still a mademoiselle?

Smeraldina: Were I already a widow, where would I find
the courage to offer both hand and heart to such a great king
to whom only the first fruits are due? Sire, I am still but
a maid.

Deramo: (looking at the Statue, now guffawing and pulling
grotesque faces) Enough, enough, Lombard Lady! None of the
beauties who have presented themselves thus far has afforded
me as much pleasure as this, of that I can assure you! Away!
Away! Withdraw! I will make my decision presently.

Smeraldina: (rising joyfully) My beloved, here, here in my
gorge I have such a sea of desires, of the most exalted, exu-
berant feelings. But to speak of these now before you, that I
cannot. I shall rather save them for the sweet hour of our
nuptials. For you should know, my beloved, how much I deify
you. Farewell! (to herself) That blow landed. He's cooked and

I'm queen. (After still more bowing and scraping, she withdraws with the little gestures of one besotted. The Guards
enter and cover up the two statues. Then they surreptitiously
swap the false statue for a true plaster cast that is iden-
tical to it in every way. Exit Smeraldina, followed by
the Guards.)

Scene 11

Deramo alone.

Deramo: (to the Statue) Fair work of art, your laughter af-
fords me so much rare wisdom, is of such rare benefit to me.
(glances at the door) See, here comes my Angela already.
I swear before heaven, I would be deeply dismayed were I now
made to see falsehood even in her. I would rather.. Oh god,
such muddled yearnings! Relentless experience robs me of
all hope! And yet... I would so much.. But I must be dream-
ing! Tell me the truth, mysterious thing!

Scene 12

Angela and Deramo.

Angela: (with noble candor) My king, see, I am here at your
command—though whether justly or not I do not know.

Deramo: (to himself) The beauty of pride! [(to Angela)] Come,
sit down, Angela! I am not unjust.

146   18

Angela: (sits down) Who, in the light of your countenance,
my king, would ever be so bold as to describe your royal com-
mands as clearly, indubitably unjust?

Deramo: Angela, you are not wanting in boldness. Speak freely
and openly and I shall not mind.

Angela: (to herself) You flatter me and take me for a fool,
cruel man! My poor heart! [(to Deramo)] What is justice to
me, my king, when, against my will, I am compelled to appear
here today even though my poor father begged that I be spared
this guessing game? I speak not for myself, for you shall
dismiss me in disgrace and I shall suffer in silence. It is
for the others out there that I speak, for those poor
wretches dutifully awaiting their disgrace. My lord, spare
them that! Make Angela the last one on whom you inflict such
pain. Forgive me, my king, but you granted me license and I
spoke with license.

Deramo: (to himself) What fair spell is this? (glancing at
the bust) The idol smiles not. Might it be true that she
alone possesses an honest heart? [(to Angela)] Angela, oh, if
only you knew the truth, you could not speak thus. For a
long, long time ago, I was looking for a faithful maid who
would love me unto death, and I never found her. But I
need an heir, which is why I invented this test. Yet now I
realize it was all in vain, all that searching.

Angela: And who is it that bears witness that not one of the
many women you have summoned is true?

Deramo: Who bears witness? That, I may not tell you. Yet now
I am sure. Do you love me, Angela?

Angela: (sighing) Sire, would it only please heaven that I did not love you!

Deramo: (looking at the bust, which does not move—to himself) The idol is still not laughing. Oh, the great joy flooding my heart! Surely it is impossible? [(to Angela)] Angela, is it true? That you could truly love me to the day I—when I, perhaps as the first... that is, before you, close my eyes forever?

Angela: Yes, my lord, I believe I could. But why do you ask? Hope... Love.... Fear... My poor heart! (weeps)

Deramo: (as above) Oh god! The Statue remains inscrutable! Is this Venetian really without falsity?

Deramo: (as above) Oh god! Love has clouded mine eyes; the truth remains hidden. (passionately) If you love me not and love another, if you cherish some secret in your breast, for pity's sake reveal it to me now, Angela, before I choose you as my wife. I cannot go on. Oh, Angela, I love you, and were I to find the tiniest falsehood in you, the pain would surely kill me!

Angela: (rising and throwing herself at his feet) Deramo, cast me out! Cast me out! What misfortune to be thus tormented! Oh, my poor heart! Oh, Deramo, have mercy on me and let me go! (weeps hot tears)

Deramo: (glancing at the unmoving Statue) Oh, dear Angela, what a rare maid you are in this evil world. Oh, weep no more! Rise! Only a scoundrel would despise such a heart. Minister! Guards! Come hither and heed my words! Let the people rejoice, for I have found a wife who loves me and who shall love me always. She is the key to my heart. (Guards enter)

Angela: No, Deramo, no! You will kill me! If you must disgrace me, then I implore you, not before your people!

Deramo: You are indeed worthy of a mighty monarch. A paragon, an exemplar of true love, you make liars of all those wicked tongues that roam the world, spreading the lie that sweet women of the Adriatic Sea are fickle and flighty and full of guile in matters of love. Come in! I have chosen Angela to be my wife.

Scene 13

Tartaglia, Pantalon, and the above.

Pantalon: (jubilant) My daughter, your majesty?

Deramo: Yes, your daughter, most richly endowed father.

Tartaglia: (furious, as an aside) Accursed hour! I am done for! I have lost Angela, and my daughter her throne.

Pantalon: Oh, your majesty! Even to such heights you wish to raise my poor daughter?

Deramo: It is to virtue that I wish to lend throne and rank.

Pantalon: It seems so impossible...

Deramo: What? You insult me! Angela, here is my hand. Be my bride, if you love me as I love you.

Angela: My king, here is mine for thee to take. With this hand, my soul is forever yours. (They give each other their hands.)

Tartaglia: (to himself) I'm angry enough to burst! (to Deramo) Beloved, revered monarch, may I ask how, after 2,748 maidens were presented to you in vain, you came to choose this Venetian?

Deramo: I shall tell you. Five years ago, that great magician Freudanalytikus entrusted me with two mysteries. Here is the one (points to the Statue) and the other I shall keep to myself. This idol here laughs at every lie. So when Angela, with her true heart, appeared before me, it pulled no ~~face~~ eyelash. (Angela looks astonished.)

Pantalon: How strange!

Tartaglia: (in a rage) So the Statue laughed at Clarissa! And my daughter is a liar! With your permission, I shall strangle her.

Deramo: Stop, Tartaglia! Clarissa loves another man. I knew it. But now, dear Angela, I am so sure, so overcome by your love and your fidelity, that I must destroy this hellish work that I may never again seek the tiniest fault in your heart. (smashes the Statue)

   (to Tartaglia) Good minister of mine, be content. Do not be unmindful of Clarissa's despondency. For now it's time to make merry! Time for a great gala hunt! Off to the forest to hunt!

Angela: I shall follow you, my king, happy, though confused. (exuent)

<u>Pantalon</u>: By my honor as a knight, I am surely dreaming. I must write to my brother Boldo in Venice of this precipitous rise in my fortunes. Letters, the postal service, the censors, and the newspapers, they shall all know of it.

<u>Tartaglia</u>: My daughter disgraced! And Angela, my Angela, lost! Oh, I feel the wrath, the envy, the ambition, the love and jealousy rising, the cancer in my bladder. A man of my qualities! I shall await my moment and avenge myself with such brilliance as theaters have never before seen, that my descendants forever after, on hearing of this will fall on their backsides in horror. (sits down on the ground)

Act 2

A room in the royal palace.

Scene 1

Tartaglia and Clarissa.

Tartaglia: Murderess, murderess! Now I've lost everything, and all because of you! You spoke of your dalliance with Leander! You threw yourself into the abyss and me with you! May you die of the plague, of cancer.......

Clarissa: No, dear father! I did not betray anything. It was the Statue that discovered my heart.

Tartaglia: Statue or no statue, heart or no heart, who gave you permission to love Leander? If you hadn't loved him, the Statue would not have laughed, imbecile!

Clarissa: Such was Leander's beauty, his eyes, his glorious words that I had no time to ask permission.

Tartaglia: If all you ever did was pay attention to all the winks and fine words of young men, you'd be in love without permission the whole time. You fool!

Clarissa: Do not insult me, father. Besides, now that Deramo has chosen another, you should console me.

Tartaglia: Console you? What? What impudence!

Clarissa: And let me marry Leander. After all, he is a cavalier and brother to the queen. So he, too, is bound to rise in rank.

Tartaglia: (furious) Listen to me! (to himself) My wrath
is giving me away. If I want revenge, I shall have to dissem-
ble. (with false amiability) Listen, my daughter, forget
what I said just now. I shall indeed console you. (to himself) Though I would rather hang you!

Clarissa: Yes, father, you shall indeed console me.

Tartaglia: Yes, yes. Now go to your room and we shall say no
more of it today.

Clarissa: I shall obey. Let me kiss your hand.

Tartaglia: Yes, yes, kiss me.... kiss whatever you want.
Good! Now go, and let me blow off a bit of steam. (He pushes
Clarissa out the door.) I'd like to slit you open like
a tench, like an eel! Doubtless the king is now with Angela.
I'll find some pretext for disturbing them. I'll tell
him it's time for the hunt. (He is about to leave when
Leander enters.)

Scene 2

Tartaglia, Leander.

Leander: Esteemed Mr. Tartaglia!

Tartaglia: What is it? I'm off to the hunt.

Leander: As, fortunately for me, the king has chosen my dear
sister to be his wife and rejected your daughter Clarissa,
I hereby declare my wish to marry her, unless you consider me
unworthy of her.

Tartaglia: As, fortunately for me, the king has chosen my
dear sister to be his wife and rejected your daughter
Clarissa........ What an outrageous thing to say! (aside) If
you are twice lucky, I am twice unlucky. You are gnawing
at my liver, you cur. — [(to Leander)] Give me three or four
days. Right now I'm busy with the affairs of state.

Leander: My dear Mr. Tartaglia, as today is a feast day.....
(sounds of hunting horns and barking hounds)

Tartaglia: That is the signal for the hunt to begin!
His majesty will have already mounted. Prepare to follow him!
Come!

Leander: You're right. I'm on my way. Where are we to hunt?

Tartaglia: Out there in front of the gates, in a forest
near the Burghölzli... (to himself) where I shall bag my
prey! (exits)

Leander: Tartaglia is a coarse fellow. He is not at
all friendly to me, yet as Clarissa's father and the king's
favorite he must be treated with prudence. (exits)

Scene 3

Truffaldin, Smeraldina.
Truffaldin pursued by Smeraldina.

Truffaldin: No, no, I will hear nothing of it.

Smeraldina: Dear little Truffaldin!

Truffaldin: Neither big nor little, neither cooked nor raw, neither stewed or roasted. No, won't. I cannot love another's leftover. Go, cast-out queen, go into the cabinet!

Smeraldina: Devilish bust!

Truffaldin: Yes, how it must have laughed when it discovered all your past affairs, your hidden flaws, those warts on your throat, the rolls of fat on your shoulders, the false teeth and false braid, the false white cotton calves, the wrinkles and the runnels under all that flour. The Statue saw them all. It sees further than your mirror. It laughed and shattered into a thousand pieces. Just like my heart........!

Smeraldina: You'll break my heart! It is Brighella's fault. It was he who threw me in there by force, who disregarded my pleas and sighs. The king himself could not hold back his tears when he saw this spectacle.

Truffaldin: But the Statue laughed. Ughh! What a rotten, ugly person!

Smeraldina: (tries to embrace him) But it was all for you, Truffaldin.

Truffaldin: Paws off, you witch! You're trying to soften my heart. But I'm not going to hunt woodcocks, nor am I going to chase a harlot.

Smeraldina: I'll follow you to the ends of the earth!

Truffaldin: No, you won't, old hen. Your women's prattle will scare away the little birds. Stay where you are.

Smeraldina: I'll follow you.

27

Truffaldin: No.

Smeraldina: Yes.

Truffaldin: No.

Smeraldina: Yes. (exuent, still bickering and hitting each other)

Scene 4

The scene changes to the forest
of Roneisloppe. The expansive view is of
a forest with mountains and a waterfall
that becomes a river. There are scattered rocks
to serve as seats. Enter Doctor Complex
with a parrot on his fist.

Complex: Here, great Freudanalytikus, my master, is the
forest of Roneisloppe.

The Parrot: Yes, Oedipus Complex. Leave me.

Complex: Adieu, Freudanalytikus.

The Parrot: I'm so great that even that soul of souls, the
fairy Urlibido, can only turn me into a creature with which I
have an affinity. Today I am a parrot and I can parrot
everything, though centuries-old things take on an exotic hue
in my beak: old meaning and new blather, an old, but eternally new truth.

Complex: Yes, get down to your great miracles and everyone
will at last understand your regression—as it is called—into
a parrot, this forest, and this little waterfall only in
the symbolic sense of all happenings and all things. I shall
await you at Schneebeli's at 7 o'clock this evening, after
the shops have closed. There we shall enjoy half a Hallauer
together and drink to the well-being of our government, to
our cheese and coal barons, the grain usurers, the deserters,
refractors, citizens, and Dadaists, and all who command us.
My Parrot, be free! (He releases the Parrot, which flies off
into the forest. Exit Dr. Complex.)

Scene 5

Deramo and Tartaglia.
Deramo enters with a shotgun slung
over his shoulder,
accompanied by Tartaglia holding
a shotgun in his hand.

Deramo: (looking at the forest) This, Tartaglia, is a
fine, spacious spot. (He turns his back on Tartaglia, who
raises his gun in readiness to shoot the king in the back.
Deramo turns round and Tartaglia lowers his gun. This
is repeated several times without Deramo becoming aware of
his minister's evil intent.)

Tartaglia: True, Your Majesty, it is indeed a fine spot.

Deramo: Yes, here we are sure to sight some game. And what a
pleasant diversion that would be. (as above)

Tartaglia: For sure. (to himself) My hand is shaking. We are alone. I could hurl him into the river.

Deramo: I have the feeling I once shot a stag on this very spot. (as above)

Tartaglia: Yes..... That's true. I remember it well. (to himself) I have soldiers nearby. I shall have Angela and the whole city seized. Yet my heart is all aflutter.

Deramo: We are alone. Where are the other hunters? (as above)

Tartaglia: (angrily) They're a long way off. Damnation! Just a moment....

Deramo: Tartaglia, you seem quite dejected and ill at ease. (leans towards him) What's the matter, my friend? What grieves you so?

Tartaglia: (to himself) Now it's too late. I'll have to await another opportunity. Never before have I been as cowardly as I am now. — [(to Deramo)] Nothing's the matter, Your Majesty.

Deramo: I can see from the way you look that you're hiding something unpleasant from me. Remember, I'm your friend and you are dear to me.

Tartaglia: (sits down; as an aside) I shall mingle falsehood with truth to prevent him becoming suspicious. [(to Deramo)] Sire, there is no longer any disguising it, I am most pro-foundly hurt.

Deramo: Why that, my friend? I shall avenge you in whichever way you wish.

Tartaglia: For thirty years I have served you faithfully, and you know very well how wisely I have counseled you in matters of war and peace; how often I have put myself on the line with the rejected princes in your bloody battles. It is true, I have been rewarded for my services, but oh, had I only met with death! Then my love for you would not have been hurt so much. (weeps)

Deramo: Who has hurt you thus, Tartaglia?

Tartaglia: For five years now, you have been in possession of the secrets of the magician Freudanalytikus. Yet despite all my services to you, you have not revealed them to me. Doubtless you have been right not to do so, but you should at least have had the grace to distinguish between me and all the others and not to expose my daughter to the ridicule of your Statue. I desire no honors nor any marks of distinction. I want only love. (weeps)

Deramo: I did you wrong, my Tartaglia. It is true, I should have trusted your heart or spared your daughter the psychoanalysis. Accept my regret for that injustice. And to prove to you how much I understand and love you, I shall now reveal to you the magician's greatest and most terrible mystery. And what a diabolical work it is! So hear, my friend, how powerful his wonder-working really is. Say this verse over any animal, over any dead person, and you yourself will die and your soul, by magic, pass into the corpse and bring it back to life, leaving your own body lifeless on the ground.

Tartaglia: What? What? So if I say this verse over a dead donkey, for example, my soul will pass into the donkey and bring it back to life? And while my own body is lying lifeless on the ground, I shall have the advantage of being a donkey? Poor Tartaglia! Your Majesty can quip at will. Your Majesty can ordain whether I live or die.

Deramo: Now you're insulting me. I'm not yet finished with the potency of this spell. If the beast into which you have passed repeats the same verse over your own corpse, your body will come back to life and the beast will drop down dead. (rising) Thus I have exposed cunning petitioners, conspirators, mischief-makers, and grievous misdeeds. By means of this miraculous power, moreover, I have punished wrongdoing and have shielded the kingdom from thieves and murderers. And now, Tartaglia, I am offering to share this rare power with you, that we may both use it, the one as also the other. So learn this spell and keep it firmly in your heart. (whispers Merlin's magic spell into Tartaglia's ear) Cra, cra, trif, traf not, agnifler canatanta siegna.

Tartaglia: (repeats it) Cra, cra, trif,........

Deramo: (repeats it) Cra, cra, trif, traf not, canatanta siegna. Now then, never again say that I love you not. (embraces him)

Tartaglia: (to himself) If this is true, oh, it could be my path to revenge and the way to win back Angela. — [(to Deramo)] My king, forgive me the wrong that I have done you. Let me... (falls to his knees)

Deramo: Rise up, dear friend. I know that your daughter loves Leander. Good, then I shall give him my island castles and Clarissa can become his wife. Thus I, too, shall right the wrong that I have done you.

Tartaglia: (to himself) And my dear Angela shall be lost to me forever! — [(to Deramo)] Magnanimous king, how can I ever repay you for such largesse?

Deramo: When you, like me, have learned that secret spell off by heart.

Tartaglia: Tric, trac, fa, fa.......

Deramo: No! Cra, cra, trif, traf not, canatanta siegna.

Tartaglia: (repeats the spell in unison with the king) Such a short verse and so damned difficult! But it may yet be of use to me. (exuent, Tartaglia behind the king, repeating the spell to himself)

Scene 6

The voices of the hunters, Pantalon, Leander,
and Brighella and the hunting horns
are heard outside. They enter in pursuit of a Bear
with their shotguns at the ready.
Brighella shoots at the Bear, which escapes:

Brighella: A hole in the water! It's all yours, Mr. Pantalon!

Pantalon: The devil take him! Watch out, I'm about to shoot! (shoots)

Brighella: Bravo! Mr. Pantalon, now he's bounding further and further away.

Pantalon: Donkey! The pan was damp. My son, he's all yours. Shoot as long as he's there to shoot.

Me, me, bravo, my suckling! He's dashing off like the devil himself.

Leander: He's wounded, he's wounded.

Pantalon: He's wounded across the forequarters. Hunter, he's all yours.

Brighella: Oh, those idiots! They've slain a hound!

Pantalon: To the hills, to the hills, and at the hillside straight up. Go hither, Brighella! And you, too, Leander, go hither. Come on!

Scene 7

Deramo and Tartaglia.

Deramo: Did you hear shots? Yet there is no one in sight.

Tartaglia: I thought (we would find a slain rhinoceros). Over there, in the distance, I can see some hunters running towards the hills.

Deramo: (looking around) Tartaglia, I can see two stags coming towards us from there. Quick, let's hide. Quick! (goes into hiding)

Tartaglia: Per bacco, how fine they are! (He goes into hiding on the other side. Two stags leap out of the forest. Deramo

34

leaves his cover, shoots, and kills one of them. Tartaglia
leaves his cover on the other side and kills the other.)

Tartaglia: Bravo, Your Majesty!

Deramo: Good shot, both of us! I shall bring this stag to my
wife as my first gift to her.

Tartaglia: (to himself) Oh, what a splendid idea! If it
works, I will have avenged myself and....... You shall
not get my Angela. Let's try. [(to Deramo)] My king, both
stags are dead.

Deramo: Yes indeed, they're no longer stirring.

Tartaglia: Since we're alone and the hunters are all
far away, might we not try out that spell of ours? For the
miracle wrought by that verse is hard to imagine.

Deramo: You're right. We could indeed. Go to one of the stags
and say the spell over it. You shall feel its effect right
away.

Tartaglia: (thoughtfully and laughing) Hmm.... Yes, yes, Your
Majesty, though I am a little scared, a little ill at ease.
Of course, if Your Majesty wishes to amuse himself....... but
I'm scared.

Deramo: Come on! That you still mistrust me I can understand
very well. So let me say the spell over this stag, while you
say it over that one. Follow me! (Deramo bends over a stag
and utters the spell.) Cra, cra, trif, traf not, sgniefler
canatanta, riogna. (Whereupon he himself slowly collapses until finally he is dead. The stag then revives, turns its
head to Tartaglia and leaps away.)

Tartaglia: What a miracle! I'm beside myself! Courage, Tartaglia, for now comes the moment of my revenge and my own happiness ever after. I shall pass into the body of the king and being regarded as king will be able to seize the realm for myself and with it the adored Angela. But what if, once I'm in that alien body, I find that my stammer has not left me? Damnation, what a dirty business that would be! Still, being king, what would I have to fear? But no more time to lose! (He utters the spell over the king's dead body and stands up again as Deramo.)

Scene 8

Tartaglia alone as Deramo.

Tartaglia: Let Deramo stew in his own misery! (stuttering) Accursed stammer! But so what? I'm king now! (to the dead Tartaglia) And you, dear body of mine, I shall make unusable by the king, King Stag, that he may not cause me any unpleasantness at court. (draws his Turkish saber and severs the head from the body, before hiding both behind a bush) My poor, unhappy body! (standing) Here come the king's ministers and hunters. First we must slay the stag in which Deramo is hiding. So great is my admiration for this cra, cra, trif, traf that only once the stag has been shot will I have nothing more to fear.

Scene 9

Enter Pantalon, Leander,
Brighella, hunters, and Tartaglia as king.
They all bow to the king,
who ceremoniously takes a seat.

Tartaglia: Quick, my lords, quick! Two stags leapt by here
just now. One of them I slew, the other escaped. Whoever
shoots the second stag for me may ask any favor of me. Away!
(exits)

Pantalon: Come on, children, come on! Do the king's bidding!
(exits)

Leander: I shall do my best to fulfill this wish. I shall
slay the stag and demand Clarissa's hand as my reward.
(exits)

Brighella: Come on, or it'll end like the hunt for the Bear,
which got away unscathed. (Outside the sounds of hunting
horns, shots being fired, cries of "Here, here it is!" The
stag leaps into view.)

Pantalon: Stay right where you are, I'm going to shoot.
(shoots and misses)

Leander: Stay right where you are, I'm going to shoot.
(shoots and misses)

Brighella: Stay right where you are, I'm going to shoot.
(shoots and misses)

Tartaglia: (angrily) Donkeys, every one of you! Clumsy
idiots! I'll beat you to death! I of all people should know

how to rid myself of useless servants. It's too late for today, but woe betide you if that stag is still alive this time
tomorrow. He who brings it to me with a red stain on its
forehead shall be rewarded with a thousand gold coins. And if
it is not caught, I'll have you all hanged. (stuttering)
But where is Tartaglia?

Pantalon: (to himself) I'm lost for words; he has become
a cur. I no longer know him. Even his voice has changed. He
stutters like Tartaglia in the most sickening way.

Tartaglia: (stuttering) But where is Tartaglia? What did you
say of Tartaglia?

Pantalon: (frankly) Nothing, nothing. Tartaglia was with Your
Majesty, was he not?

Tartaglia: True, but I lost sight of him a long time ago.

Leander: The city is not far from here; perhaps he is there.

Tartaglia: Yes, yes, perhaps, but I know how much this
minister is despised simply because I love him so, and would
not want him to meet with any sad misfortune. (stuttering
and forgetting himself)

Pantalon: Death and the devil take me! What an art of stuttering is this!

Tartaglia: (to himself) My stammer haunts me still. I did not
want... But what have I to fear? (to the hunters) Remember,
if the slain deer is not brought to me tomorrow, I'll have
the gallows put up. (exits)

Pantalon: Let's go! I'm so tired that my knees have turned to jelly, and so shocked by the strange new things that I have seen that I could run off to Venice like a footman. (exits)

Leander: Brighella, if I had slain the stag, Clarissa would be mine. (exits)

Brighella: This little lord has nothing but love in his skull, and as for me, it seems my head is full of those medlars that might otherwise fill a stag's belly. (exits)

Scene 10

Deramo as stag. The stag enters.

Deramo: Thank you, great Jupiter, for having liberated me from such frightful peril, though you have now condemned me to live as a beast. Unhappy me, to be pursued by hounds and hunters! (contemplates himself in the water) Is this grotesque face Deramo's? Tartaglia, you traitor! Is this your thanks for everything that I have done for you? I can almost feel you holding Angela in your arms. I must return to my castle and my precious wife this very evening. I know of a secret little gate in the park by which I can swiftly bypass the servants and the guard dogs. But will she recognize the husband she loves in this horned beast? Courage, dear heart! If heaven abandons me, I shall meet with death soon enough. (exits)

Scene 11

Truffaldin, alone. He enters with a bird
net that he proceeds to install.

Truffaldin: This is a good spot for my hunt. Night will soon
fall, and then all the little birdies will fly back to the
nest. Here's a pretty net for you, my little ones: Peep
peep..... Oh look, a dead deer. That must be the one demanded
by the king. Ten thousand pieces! What a stroke of luck! Now,
Smeraldina will be mine! But wait, Truffaldin. Remember how
ungrateful she was. No, I've had enough of her and want nothing more to do with her. Hush! Now the birds are flying home.
How the forest is murmuring! And I, too, shall play my symphony. (whistles comically) Truly, I have no need of a large
orchestra. Look there, a great bird! (The bird motif from
"Siegfried" is heard and a parrot flies onto the stage.) Is
it a stork? No, it is white and red after the latest fashion.
Psst.... Psst.... Here! (whistling) He's approaching the
net... But no, the rascal's not going to go there.... or is
he? Ha! Now he's snared. (jumps up and traps the Parrot
inside the net)

Scene 12

Freudanalytikus as Parrot
and Truffaldin.

The Parrot: Truffaldin!

Truffaldin: Who calls? Who's that hiding behind me? Not that
I'm afraid, no, not at all. There, in the bush, I can see

you very well. Don't you want to come out? But what's this?
A body without a head? Can that be Tartaglia? Argh! I'm off,
I'm scared, I'm scared.

The Parrot: Truffaldin, fear not!

Truffaldin: It cannot be the corpse, so..... it must be this
bird. (strokes it)

Truffaldin: (continuing) Coco, coco, did you breakfast well?

The Parrot: Bring me to the court of the queen.

Truffaldin: To the court? To the queen?

The Parrot: Yes, for then you will be rich, rich, rich.

Truffaldin: Rich, rich? That's a lot of riches all at once.
The stag, the Parrot, and now Tartaglia! And how am I sup-
posed to carry all of this to the court? Hey, you there, come
and help me. Night is falling. Help me take away this
baggage! (He struggles with the cage. The Parrot shrieks.)

The Parrot: Rich, Truffaldin, rich, rich.

Act 3

A hall in the royal palace

Scene 1

Tartaglia as king and Angela.
Tartaglia pursues Angela, who is fleeing from him.
He is behaving like a coarse peasant
and stuttering constantly.

Angela: (miserably) Oh, leave me in peace!

Tartaglia: The devil I will! How you have changed, dear heart! How tenderly I have been following you this past hour, but all in vain. You have seemingly gone mad. Not once in this long hour have I been able to so much as touch your hand. (babbles on while Angela stares at him in amazement, especially every time he stutters.) (to himself) How she's staring at me! Does she know? Oh no, that's impossible! Beloved, have you nothing to say? What became of your great love?

Angela: (with emotion) Oh god, Deramo, don't be angry with me if I speak openly with you.

Deramo [sic]: To hell with it, then speak openly!

Angela: (rising) Oh king, you must know that I no longer find Deramo in you.

Tartaglia: What? How so? Why? Damnation! And again, damnation!

Angela: I do not know. (staring at him) And yet, you are him.
I see your proud countenance and your body that so recently
aroused love in me. But your gestures are no longer the same,
nor your mind, nor your heart, nor your soaring thoughts.
I no longer find them in you. And not finding them pains me
greatly.

Tartaglia: Come now, you are just imagining it. You have
succumbed to hysteria, a disease of the brain. I shall have
you bled.

Angela: Let me hide myself in my room and weep..........

Tartaglia: Then go! This will pass. Soon you will love me all
over again. (Angela exits, weeping.)

Scene 2

Tartaglia alone.

Tartaglia: This calls for calm, though I feel the love in me
rising to a frenzy. First prayers, sugar sweetness, and flattery, and then force and revenge. And there's still arsenic,
murder, and blood for all who resist me.

Tartaglia, Clarissa.

Clarissa: Justice, good king, for pity's sake do me justice.
(She weeps hot tears.)

Tartaglia: What's the matter, Clarissa?

Clarissa: Oh, my poor father, your head severed from your
body! (weeps)

Tartaglia: Poor girl, I do feel sorry for her. Which miscre-
ants did this deed?

Clarissa: We don't know. How unhappy I am. (weeps)

Tartaglia: (to himself) She stirs my heart. But I shall keep
my secret....... (aloud) I shall catch those murderers! Leave
me alone now.

Clarissa: Sir, I shall obey and place my faith in you.
(exits, weeping)

Scene 4

Pantalon, Leander, Tartaglia.

Leander: (animatedly) King Deramo, such a sad event!

Pantalon: Oh, Your Majesty, poor Tartaglia!

Tartaglia: (arrogantly) I know all. Who brought the news?

Pantalon: Truffaldin, the birdcatcher.

Tartaglia: Hey! Guards! (Guards enter) Throw Truffaldin into prison and with him all those who were on the hunt. Disarm Leander and Pantalon and throw them into the deepest dungeon you have. We shall commence work on the murder charge against these two right away.

Leander: Disarm me?

Pantalon: Me, Your Majesty?

Tartaglia: (to the Guards) Obey. Take them to the tower. And if they are blameless, you can take them down again. (to himself) Where is that accursed stag? Angela, beware. I am now the ruler here. (exits)

Leander: I've lost all hope.

Pantalon: So these are my first dividends as the king's father-in-law. It is a dubious profit. (The Guards take them away.)

Scene 5

The royal chamber.
A pedestal with a parrot perched
on it in the background.

Deramo: (as stag) Oh what a sad fate for a young husband, to have to cross the threshold of his home as a stag! Will I

ever see her again? Will she believe me? I am risking my
life. I hear voices. Where shall I hide? (He hides in the
room on the left. Enter Angela and Truffaldin.)

Scene 6 [1]

Angela, Truffaldin.

Angela: (at first to herself) Tartaglia dead, and my father
and brother in captivity! What a sudden change of fortune,
what grief! And Deramo, too, is no longer himself. But who is
there? (In the background, the stag pokes its head into the
room and on hearing Truffaldin withdraws again.)

Truffaldin: (entering on tiptoe) It is I, fair lady, I,
Truffaldin. I do most humbly beg your pardon for having been
so tardy in paying tribute to you and bringing you my cage.
It is a bird, Your Majesty, and I did not want..... A very
modest gift, though the bird be rare, fine, and wise.

Angela: Leave me, Truffaldin. I have other things in my head
besides your bird and your foolery. Leave me!

Truffaldin: Have you even seen my Parrot? He is so wise and
learned, and as virtuous as any polymath; and more talka-
tive than all the women in the world. He talks and talks and
talks, like a lawyer, like a socialist. (approaching the
cage) Coco, coco, want to give us a little lecture? Her Majesty will see that he has a voice as mellifluous as a priest.
He is quite the cosmopolitan and speaks more languages than
a hotel doorman: Italian, Russian, German, English, Dutch,
French, American, Spanish, Chinese, Zurich dialect, and hence

Dada. Coco, coco, you'll get su-sugar or at least saccharine. Now, of course, the oaf won't answer. He's swallowed his tongue. I beg Your Majesty's patience; he's as gentle as a pacifist. Won't you speak to us, accursed creature?

Angela: Go! Otherwise I'll have you thrown from my balcony.

Truffaldin: That could kill me! Damned Parrot! (Guard enters)

Guard: Pardon me, great lady!

Angela: What, a guard in my room?!

Truffaldin: Fear not, Your Majesty. Doubtless this person was sent to me personally by the king. He is to recompense me for catching the stag. So where are the ten thousand pieces?

Guard: Fool, off to prison with you! You're the murderer.

Angela: You dare to march into my chamber?

Guard: On the king's orders, Ma'am. Now follow me, you arch-rogue.

Truffaldin: What a fine reward. A curse on all of them, the Parrot, the stag, the king, and the queen. (to the Guard pulling him along) Stop, not so rough, I'm innocent.

Guard: Away with you. Just be glad I'm not being even rougher. (He leads him away.)

Scene 6 [2]

Angela alone, later joined
by Deramo as stag.

<u>Angela</u>: Oh, the tyrant has unmasked himself. How lamentable my situation has become. (weeps)

<u>Voice of the king</u>: Beloved, weep not.

<u>Angela</u>: What is that I hear? The voice of the king?

<u>Voice of the king</u>: Yes, the voice of he who will love you forever.

<u>Angela</u>: Can it be? (The stag appears.) Oh heavens! A stag!

<u>Deramo</u>: Fear not! It is I, Deramo, by a wicked spell turned into a stag.

<u>Angela</u>: And the other Deramo?

<u>Deramo</u>: Is just a deception. Angela, my beloved, let us bewail our misfortune. Tartaglia was the one who stole my body's magic power, and with it perhaps your love.

<u>Angela</u>: No, never, for a subtle inkling shielded my virtue for me. Hush, someone is coming. Hide in my chamber. There we shall plan our vengeance.

<u>Deramo</u>: Oh, what bliss! (exuent into the room on the left)

Scene 7

Smeraldina and Brighella.
Brighella, with Smeraldina
in hot pursuit.

Brighella: You bore me, you disgust me. And if it continues thus, I shall kick you out of the house. Has the devil taken possession of you?

Smeraldina: Yes, yes, you traitor! Your ambition has ruined me. You begged me to enter the king's cabinet, and now Truffaldin wants nothing more to do with me. My honor has been forfeited, and with it many a fine proposal. If you don't find me a husband now, I shall become a veritable satan in your house.

Brighella: Oh, go to hell and find a husband yourself! You're good enough for that. Auction yourself off, put an advertisement in the *Tagesanzeiger*.

Smeraldina: Suits me, donkey! I've done all that anyway: have shaken hands with every footman in town, have turned the eyes of every saucier, have sighed on every stable boy. But they all acted disgusted and pulled faces, and only because the king rejected me.

Brighella: You want to know the real reason they pulled faces at you? What has really hurt your prospects?

Smeraldina: How? What? What? You who have robbed me of my honor, of my well-being.

Brighella: That you are over forty. And more hideous than original sin. What really hurts your prospects, and mine—

I can no longer keep this from you—is your folly in pretend-
ing to be a mere maid, whereas everyone here knows that back
in Lombardy, you served more than six different houses as
a wet nurse. So enough of that, giant cow! (exits in a rage)

Smeraldina: Donkey, traitor, dog! (She runs after him to
strike him.)

The Parrot: Oh, women, women! Pity him who is burdened with
them. Praise him who sees through them. (The Parrot flaps
its wings. Angela emerges from her chamber and speaks to the
concealed stag.)

Scene 8

Angela: (to the invisible Deramo) Keep yourself hidden
and have no fear. I shall do everything we agreed. Trust me,
for even virtue, at least when it loves, knows a thousand
tricks. (She reclines on the divan and pretends to sleep;
enter Tartaglia, followed by Guards.)

Tartaglia: I've eclipsed them all yet am still mistrustful.
What of it—I alone am king and they all fear me. (seeing
Angela) Only this heart is missing from my happiness. Yet I
am wracked by love, so must try again. [(to Angela)] Have
you now been fully cured of that hysteria that took you away
from me?

Angela: My lord, I pray to God that He deliver me from the
deceit that made me so downcast and so wretched. My resist-
ance to you is dissipating.

Tartaglia: Splendid, my beloved! (taking her hand)

Angela: (to herself) Disgraceful traitor! [(to Tartaglia)]
But why, disregarding my tender feelings, were my father
and brother thrown into prison? Is that truly your desire,
Deramo? (weeps)

Tartaglia: Weep not, my sun, my moon! Tartaglia's death so
agitated the people that it was done only to calm them down.
But I shall prove my love to you forthwith. Guards! Release
Leander and Pantalon!

Angela: I already feel my love growing.

Tartaglia: (fervently) Apple of mine eye, you can ask anything of me and I shall fulfill your every wish.

Angela: (softly) The soldiers, Deramo.

Tartaglia: (to the Guards) Go, and return only at my signal.
(The Guards leave.) At last we are alone, Angela. (kneeling)

Angela: Your heart proved your love for me this morning,
Deramo. You spoke of some magic power by which a human soul
might be transplanted into a dead body. I beg you, therefore,
perform this one feat before me.

Tartaglia: (rising, to himself) Deramo has spoken. A states-
man keeps his secrets to himself.

Angela: You hesitate?

Tartaglia: Listen to me, dear wife! I do indeed know the most
magnificent secrets for our wedding night. And tomorrow,
if you wish, I shall take you to the stag carcass brought to

me by Truffaldin. See, my soul must first have passed through yours.

Angela: (standing up) Fulfill this wish of mine and I am yours.

Tartaglia: (seizing her) Enough chatter! Do your duty!

Angela: (crying out) Oh Deramo, I implore you!

Tartaglia: (dragging her away) There'll be no more imploring now.

Angela: Help, help, Deramo.

Scene 9

Deramo: (still outside) Traitor! Not one step more.

Tartaglia: The voice of the king! I am undone! (to Angela) You hid a murderer for me! Hey, guards! Hey there! (He exits in a hurry and returns with a drawn saber.)

Deramo: (as stag) Well might you quake at your impending punishment, Tartaglia!

Tartaglia: Oh horrid, horned monster, hellish beast, die at my hand!

Deramo: A battle? Bring it on! I accept the challenge. (Tartaglia and the stag engage in battle.)

Tartaglia: Coward, you're scared! (Thunder, an earthquake. The stag and Tartaglia cease fighting. The Parrot shrieks.)

Freudanalytikus: (as Parrot) Urlibido, you, the most primal of all our drives, to all your miracles now add this: Fall away, feathers! So that naked and innocent as the spirit itself, I may hasten to aid innocence. (The Parrot changes into Freudanalytikus, who again becomes the famous professor, clad in the fashion of the day and with a little cane in his hand.)

Angela: Heavens!

Deramo: What a wonder!

Tartaglia: What? But what's this? Why? I'm all atremble. Hey, Guards!

Freudanalytikus: (to Deramo) When all is driven to destruction, the soul gripped by madness, people fighting each other like devils, then only one power can help. It is a power that no one knows but everyone can name: faith in science, knowing fog from clarity, pitch from sulfur, deception from truth. You fear nothing, since you are as innocent as I am. (to Tartaglia) But you fear everything, you rogue and crook! With such a soul wanting to be king! Only he who analyzes his soul and smooths out every fold in it with the power of our wise wonderworks—only he can hope to match me. Exchange the bodies. Let each soul dwell where it belongs. (He raises his wand and the stag turns back into Deramo, now clad in gorgeous raiments. Tartaglia returns to his erstwhile form, but clad only in a nightshirt full of holes with his bare skin peeping through.)

Angela: (throwing herself into the king's arms) My Deramo!

Deramo: Angela!

Tartaglia: Where should I hide? I am naked, my libido visible far and wide.

Freudanalytikus: Stop, miscreant! You shall die of shame!

Final Scene

The whole cast,
including the people and Guards.

Everyone: Tartaglia, Tartaglia!

Tartaglia: Kill me, kill me! I did not analyze myself and can no longer do it now. So kill me!

Freudanalytikus: Ridicule never killed anyone in this city, so die instead of my wrath! (Tartaglia falls down dead and is carried off. Clarissa weeps. Leander comforts her.)

Pantalon: None of this makes sense, no sense at all.

Deramo: It was all a misunderstanding, as a politician would say. But now I shall take Angela, Leander Clarissa, and Truffaldin whomsoever he pleases, and we shall all be merry again.

For if the king is happy, the people are too. And if the people are happy, the king is too. And it is the great, most profound Freudanalytikus, we have to thank for all the happiness on earth!

<u>Freudanalytikus</u>: You have seen the wonders of my powers.
Urlibido, the salt in every sap, soon turns man into beast.
You live in me and in my brothers, in all who are true to
me and all who are mine enemies. And should you not know
where to go, despite what you have just now seen, despite
this highly symbolic tale, then go to all three and be young
and of good cheer, and learn to fly again; be swift as a
boisterous young eagle, for that is the purpose of life, to
find you, Urlibido, and it is my wisdom's most sacred duty to
find you in every form and in every person. And just as
everyone likes to see the beast still lurking in every human
heart, how kings can be led by the nose as much as can the
blind, how the finest soul is still driven by animal instincts and still stinks of sulfur, so I know that this play
has indeed pleased you. Farewell, and do not forget what
you have just seen. Do not leave it too late with analysis!
Do not leave it too late to dance to this tune!

APPLAUSE

MEDEA HOCH

KING STAG—DADA ON THE WERKBUND STAGE[1]

HOW MODERNISM
AND THE SWISS PUPPET THEATER
REDISCOVERED MARIONETTES

The puppet theater production of an updated version of Carlo Gozzi's fairy-tale drama *Il re cervo* (*King Stag*) was conceived for the Swiss Werkbund exhibition in Zurich, held during the last summer of the war, from May 18 to September 15, 1918 [fig. 1]. The Schweizerisches Marionettentheater (Swiss Puppet Theater) that the Swiss Werkbund had founded specifically for this occasion had a program comprising nine works altogether, some old, some new, one an opera, another a ballet. The three performances of *King Stag* on September 11, 12, and 13 were "a great success," in the words of Sophie Taeuber-Arp, the creator of both the marionettes and the stage sets; yet they would not have taken place at all had the exhibition not been extended.[2] On July 28, director Werner Wolff had informed the chairman of the Swiss Werkbund's Marionettes Committee, Werner Reinhart, that owing to poor audience numbers, the heat, and the spread of the Spanish flu, the puppet theater would be suspended as of August 13 and that "the ballet and King Stag"[3] would not be rehearsed at all, even though "the stage sets and puppets were finished." Exactly why *King Stag* was put on after all, and especially after the management, according to Taeuber-Arp, had declared her production "much too modern and too audacious,"[4] is impossible to say.

The exhibition building on Sechseläutenplatz in Zurich had been designed by Alfred Altherr, director of Zurich's Gewerbeschule (Trade School) and chairman of the Swiss Werkbund that he had co-founded in 1913. He

[fig. 1]   Otto Morach, poster design for the Swiss
Werkbund puppet theater, 65 × 44.5 cm,
1918

had the puppet theater—launched at his instigation—situated in the middle of the horseshoe-shaped complex [fig. 2]. The creation of a puppet theater for Zurich had been a matter close to his heart ever since 1914. It was then that his *Theaterkunst* exhibition at the Kunstgewerbemuseum (Museum of Arts and Crafts, now Museum für Gestaltung Zürich) highlighting the work of the reformers Adolph Appia and Edward Gordon Craig had featured Burmese and Javanese puppets, marionettes from Craig's own workshop, and even a guest performance by Paul Brann's Munich-based puppet theater, the Marionetten-Theater Münchner Künstler [fig. 3]. Altherr's undertaking had the professional support of Hermann Scherrer, a city councillor of St. Gallen, whose own St. Galler Marionettentheater, founded in 1903, was Switzerland's oldest permanent puppet theater. Altherr was also able to recruit the businessman and patron of New Music, Werner Reinhart of Winterthur, to chair the Werkbund's new Marionettes Committee. It was thanks to Reinhart that in 1919 the Kunstgewerbemuseum was able to acquire the "stage equipment, decorations, and marionettes" of the Schweizerisches Marionettentheater.[5] The writer Werner Wolff, who was a personal friend of Reinhart and at the time was working as a dramatist for the Stadttheater Bern, was engaged to direct all nine plays. Some years earlier, he had already tried to establish a Swiss puppet theater.[6]

Altherr had geared the work of the trade school's arts and crafts department to reformist principles. Figural theater thus became an important field of experimentation, in that it enabled reformers to test *Gesamtkunstwerk* projects and to develop models for abstract-style stage sets, while at the same time offering

"good" entertainment for children and adults alike.[7] Altherr saw figural theater both as a "lifeline" against realistic theater and cinema and as a "composite of all the arts."[8] The sculptor Carl Fischer, who taught modeling and carving at the same school, likewise emphasized the collaborative character of this form of theater, describing it as "a collective effort on the part of teachers, pupils, artists."[9]

For avant-garde artists, too, figural theater proved to be a valuable platform for experimentation with new forms of abstract design. Indeed, every avant-garde movement of the 1910s and 1920s had projects of its own in this genre. The Futurists, for example, staged Fortunato Depero's *Balli plastici* (1918) and Enrico Prampolini's *Matoum et Tévibar* (1918); the Constructivists produced plays by Vladimir Sokoloff, Ladislav Sutnar, Natalia Goncharova, Mikhail Larionov, and Alexandra Exter; at the Bauhaus, Ilse Fehling created stick puppets while Alma Siedhoff-Buscher designed a toy cupboard with built-in puppet theater; and finally, among the Dadaists, Emmy Hennings designed hand puppets, Hannah Höch Dada dolls, and Sophie Taeuber-Arp the marionettes for *King Stag*. Thus, it was the popular genre of puppet theater that gave many people from all walks of life their first encounter with avant-garde art.

THE RENEWAL OF
MARIONETTE DESIGN AND UPDATING
OF A BAROQUE PLAY

Sophie Taeuber-Arp received her training as an artist in St. Gallen and Munich, both of them cities with exceptionally lively puppet theaters. That she was interested in marionettes even as a student is evident from a letter she wrote to her sister from Munich: "When you visit the trade show, be sure to go to the puppet theater. The only thing worth seeing in the large main hall, apart from the decorations, are the artist dolls, as the rest is just kitsch and some of it very poor indeed."[10] Taeuber-Arp already had some first-hand experience of the stage; not only had she been a student at Rudolf von Laban's Schule für Bewegungskunst (School for the Art of Movement) in Zurich but she had also danced at various Dada soirées (see the essay by Christina Thurner, pp. 224 ff.). She had been a teacher of design and embroidery in the arts and crafts department of Zurich's trade school since 1916, and a member of the Swiss Werkbund since 1915; furthermore, she was the only woman to be appointed to the Werkbund's Marionettes Committee.[11] One of her chief responsibilities in that capacity was to oversee the production of the test piece *Die Zaubergeige* (Magic Fiddle) by Franz von Pocci, and to recruit puppet masters to manipulate the puppets.[12] She also proposed the applied artist Johanna Fülscher for the demanding task of staging Claude Debussy's ballet *La boîte à joujoux* (The Toy-Box), though Fülscher passed up the opportunity in favor of Otto Morach.[13]

Taeuber-Arp's choice of Carlo Gozzi's tragicomic blend of oriental folktale and commedia dell'arte, *Il re cervo* of 1762, as preferable to all the other works proposed at the committee meeting held on January 15, 1918, presumably had to do with the way fairy tales represent an abstract world, a quality that Novalis had remarked on in the piece "Aufzeichnungen des *Allgemeinen Brouillon.*"[14] She seems to have detected a kindred spirit in Gozzi, who certainly waxed polemical in his attacks on Carlo Goldoni's realistic theater; and during a stay in Arosa in 1919, she wrote a detailed report on E. T. A. Hoffmann's "Seltsame Leiden eines Theaterdirektors" (1818). In one of the dialogues in that work, a theater director mentions staging Gozzi's *King Stag* with an ensemble of marionettes. "That Hoffmann of all people had claimed Gozzi for the marionettes," wrote Taeuber-Arp, "pleased me very much."[15]

At its meeting in January 1918, the committee commissioned various artists with the production of the puppet plays on the exhibition program. It also entrusted René Morax and Werner Wolff, both of whom had puppet plays of their own on the program, with a modern reworking of Gozzi's *Il re cervo*.[16] It was probably Reinhart, who was well-connected in French-speaking Switzerland, who invited the Vaudois Morax, a playwright and founder of the Théâtre du Jorat in Mézières, to collaborate with the committee. After all, he had previously supported Morax's book *Théâtre de poupées*, published by Cahiers Vaudois in 1917.[17] And presumably it was again Reinhart who proposed a production of *King Stag* for the Werkbund exhibition. He borrowed the Italian original along with the German translation produced during Gozzi's lifetime from the Zentralbibliothek Zurich and sent them both to Morax. It was the latter version that Taeuber-Arp began working with in February 1918, at least until the modern adaptation was delivered in mid-March. When Morax sent Reinhart his updated French translation of the work, he remarked: "Ce sera une pièce très vivante et très gaie, mais difficile à monter" ("It'll be a very lively and very gay piece, but difficult to stage").[18]

This new version is set in Zurich in 1918 and parodies psychoanalysis as a form of magic. Since Morax,

Wolff, and Taeuber-Arp all sat on the Marionettes Committee, presumably they agreed in advance on this satirical slant. Taeuber-Arp had a connection to Jung through her sister, Erika Schlegel, who was a member of his Psychological Club and its librarian. Wolff derived his German version of the play from Morax's French one.[19] In late February 1918, he informed Reinhart that most of the updating of the piece was based on Morax's version,[20] as is borne out by a comparison between the two. The French version is altogether more detailed and more explicit,[21] and while Wolff certainly tightened it up somewhat, he also added some completely new passages, most of them in the second half of the play. These openly poke fun at psychoanalytical concepts such as regression and libido,[22] especially in Freudanalytikus' final soliloquy. Wolff also accentuated the role of Zurich as the scene of the action, for example by adding allusions to the "Dadaists" and the *Tagesanzeiger* (a local newspaper).

While Morax and Wolff were updating this eighteenth-century drama, Taeuber-Arp was busy creating modernist marionettes and stage sets. Her turned figurines are very different from the carved and clothed puppets that had typically been used hitherto. They are composed of stereometric wooden elements, which the sculptor Carl Fischer had made with a woodturner after the artist's very precise construction drawings and then assembled for her.[23] The artist then took care of the characterization by painting the figures in two or three different colors, in most cases confining herself to one color per element. The brass parts were produced by a goldsmith.[24] Whereas the turned marionettes and props are conceived wholly in the round, the stage set "King's Cabinet" is two-dimensional. Jean Arp regarded the image as a pioneering work of Constructivist art, and in a letter of 1949 asked Hans Richter to settle the "never-ending dispute over the dates of the first abstract images" sparked by Michel Seuphor's exhibition *L'art abstrait. Ses origines, ses premiers maîtres* at the Galerie Maeght in Paris, by referring readers to the photograph of that particular scene published in *Das Werk* in August 1918.[25]

The exact turning technique—which Marcel Duchamp, in his portrait of Sophie Taeuber-Arp, praised as a "consciously accurate technique"[26]—makes for a sharp contrast with the uncontrolled movements of the marionettes, most of which were suspended only by their heads and hands. The willowy wooden limbs, connected by visible brass eye bolts, moved in an unnaturally tremulous way in all directions. Jean Arp had already noticed how the marionettes evoked the aesthetic of Taeuber-Arp's own abstract dances (see the essay by Christina Thurner, pp. 224 ff.) and remarked: "Ce que Hugo Ball a écrit de la danse de Sophie Taeuber peut être répété à propos des marionnettes qu'elle exécuta à cette époque" ("What Hugo Ball said of Sophie Taeuber's dance might also be said of the marionettes she was making at the time").[27]

They certainly do not depict people, and as Max Bill noted, unlike other such puppets, "they were concerned less with the physiognomic expressiveness of the head than with the typical expressiveness of the figures composed of certain formal elements."[28] The figures' social and kinship bonds are rendered visible by means of both formal and chromatic correspondences. King Deramo, his bride Angela, and King Stag, for example, all have golden pupils; the king and his two ministers, Tartaglia and Pantalon, all wear mantles; Freudanalytikus and his alter ego the Parrot are painted the same pastel colors, while Freudanalytikus and his pupil Dr. Complex resemble each other in their elongated bodies, short legs, similar headgear, conical hands and feet, and the absence of textile accessories; Pantalon and his children Angela and Leander wear conical hats, are clad in similar colors, and have spherical feet; the would-be king Tartaglia and his daughter Clarissa share the color cinnabar, which is also the color of the throne; the brother and sister Brighella and Smeraldina are painted ocher and two shades of blue, and both have protruding ears, painted-on noses and the same shaped hands; as a couple, Truffaldin and Smeraldina share the color ocher and their love of feathers as ornaments.

The three stage sets have unfortunately been lost, though Taeuber-Arp's staging can still be reconstructed. What have survived are the seventeen marionettes with almost all the props, twenty-four construction drawings for the puppets, done in pencil, and five small-format design drawings for the stage sets done in colored crayon. To these can be added the thirteen historical photos by Ernst Linck. A comparison between the marionettes and the drawings shows that the figures underwent further abstraction as they were being made. The Guards and the Statue, for example, were not given faces after all, and some of the details in the sheet brass were omitted. The stage sets can be ascertained from a comparison of the colored design drawings [pp. 1–7] with the photos taken of the relevant scenes [pp. 34–41].[29] Also revealing are Taeuber-Arp's own descriptions on the versos of some of the photos, one of which reads: "The King's Cabinet. In many shades of red, mainly cinnabar. The light patches are silvered. At first, these flecks of silver are all that can be seen in the dim light of the transfiguration scene. Then the room begins to softly glow, eventually becoming a radiant red."[30]

THE MARIONETTES AS ICONS OF DADAISM

The importance of puppet theater to modernism is also evident in the attentiveness of the reviews that were published in various newspapers and journals. Unlike the write-ups of the other performances staged as part of the Swiss Werkbund exhibition, the discussions of *King Stag* covered not just the content of the play but also the modernity of the production. Writing for the journal *Das Werk*, Waldemar Jollos, for example, wrote: "The tradition that, no matter how fantastical, still has audiences squinting back at the forms of reality, no longer counts here. [...] The novelty is that all [figures] are parts of a single work of art and were born of one idea."[31] In September 1918, the *Neue Zürcher Zeitung* reported as follows: "It is not least the artistic mise-en-scène that has made this piece such a success; because it offers something wholly new. The grotesque, a quality intrinsic to puppetry that lends it much of its quintessential charm, at least up to a point, is effectively enhanced by the differently sized puppets, their deliberately exaggerated proportions—say, of the arms—and the fantastical outfits that they wear."[32] And the *Züricher Post* for its part commented: "In contrast to the illusionistic design of most marionette plays, here an attempt was made to make the fairy-tale-like quality of the doll-like figures almost palpable."[33]

There were more enthusiastic reviews when Paul Brann's Marionetten-Theater Münchner Künstler was a guest of the Kunstgewerbemuseum Zürich during its exhibition *Marionetten und Schattenspielfiguren* held from February 8 to March 21, 1920. Of all the works in the repertoire of the Schweizerisches Marionettentheater it could have played, it chose to revive *King Stag*. "These figurines by Miss Sophie H. Taeuber are truly burlesque inventions. How exquisite the impact of those body-guards, those conjoined people, no longer individuals, more an automaton. Or this monster from Lombardy who calls herself Smeraldina. And the excellent 'Freud-analytikus'! The crazy corporeality of the figurines en-hances our impression of their belonging to a fantastical sphere. The puppet theater makes a joke out of a revolu-tion in its staging, alongside which real theaters, come across as conservative court theaters,"[34] wrote the *Neue Zürcher Zeitung*, while the *Züricher Post* once again ad-dressed the modernity of the designs: "The cubist pup-pets, as curious as they are comical, did not miss their mark this time round either. What makes them so special is that it is precisely their fantastical design that gives the spectators' imagination so much to work on."[35]

Despite being performed as part of an event showcasing Swiss arts and crafts, the production of *King Stag* became an icon of Dadaism. The artist herself prompted this reception by reproducing the figure of Freudanalytikus in the Dadaist magazine *Der Zeltweg* in 1919. In an article titled "New Marionettes" (1919) pub-lished in the Berlin-based magazine *Die Dame,* Otto Flake remarked that not only was Taeuber "venturing down new paths with her decorations and figures" but that she was "already presenting definitive solutions."[36] In 1919–1920, when Richard Huelsenbeck and Kurt Wolff were planning and collecting material for their Dadaist

68

What We Are Doing in Europe

Some Account of the Latest Ballets, Books, Pictures and Literary Scandals of the Continent

By TRISTAN TZARA

A tragic scene from the "Count of Monte Cristo" sketched by Jean Cocteau

Serge de Diaghilev and Nijinski. A caricature by Jean Cocteau

IGOR STRAVINSKY
A new portrait of the celebrated modernist composer by Robert Delaunay. Stravinsky's latest ballet, "Mavra", which has proved as startling to the critics as this composer's previous works, is discussed on another page by Jean Cocteau

A Dadaist marionette, now performing at Zurich. An officer of high rank but of tragic stupidity

"The Bird Catcher" —another revolutionary marionette. He is equipped with a set of rings for birds

Le Rossignol Chinois, a portrait study by Max Ernst, one of the most prominent of the Dadaists

THE June season in Paris, practically every year, includes a series of performances by the Russian Ballet. This year the productions took place at the Opera and at the Théâtre Nogador. The Russian Ballet brought us several novelties and the proof that its d i r e c t o r, Serge de Diaghilev, is still in possession of his s u r e vitalizing power.

The Marriage of Sleeping Beauty is a ballet embroidered on an old folk tale and set to subtle and inventive music by Tchaikovsky. His score seems to me, however, rather sentimental and sweet. But, not being a connoisseur, I rely on the judgment of Stravinsky, who declares it very beautiful. The settings a n d costumes are by Madam Gontcharoona.

Madame Nijinska, the sister of Nijinski, is the present soul of the Russian Ballet. A precise fantasy, strange and marvellous facial expressions and graceful but powerful movements animate her body. She dances the part of the Cat in the *Sleeping Beauty*, a prodigious and impish cat.

The culminating point of the ballet is at the end, where Madame Trílova, an incomparable dancer, lightly executes thirty-two continuous pirouettes on the tip of her toes. Here is what Mr. A. Levinson, a specialist in ballet dancing, writes about this feat:

"For a half century the great Italian virtuosi had held the first place in the imperial stage, the Théâtre Marie of Petrograd. The last Italian star was Pierina Legnani, who thrilled the ballet enthusiasts of the capital by executing in this coda of Tschaikovsky twenty-four pirouettes. The years had rendered this tour de force a great mem-

ory, when Tríplova, a young première danseuse, dancing this same finale, executed thirty-two pirouettes with the same simplicity, the same reserved grace, that we admire in her today. By this symbolic gesture, the Russian ballet was definitely freed from foreign domination: its own supremacy became indisputable, and soon w a s u n d i s- puted."

"The Fox"

ANOTHER ballet, The Fox, is founded on a well known Fable; for it Igor Stravinsky has written music which is curious and fervently rich— m u s i c which proves to us once more that he is one of the great composers of our t i m e. Four s i n g e r s placed in the orchestra sing the rôles of the four dancers on the stage. One of them shouts at a certain moment when the music pauses: "But what is all this music?" This produces an irresistible effect. At the end of the ballet one hears the same voice announcing, "If our story has pleased you, please pay us our due."

The action of the ballet takes place in a barnyard. The cock is roosting. In order to get him off his perch, the fox employs all sorts of stratagems and finally appears disguised as a nun. He tries to sieze the fox, but the cat and the ram come to the latter's assistance. After various tumblings, which are a stylized simplification of dancing, the fox retires.

Madame Nijinska's choreography adapts itself marvelously to this clumsy and childish peasant talk. The designs for scenery and costumes were made by the Russian painter, Larionov, who is a frequent collaborator with M. Diaghilev in the

(Continued on page 100)

world atlas *Dadaco*, which would never actually be published, the artist offered them Ernst Linck's photo of the marionette Truffaldin. Tristan Tzara's glamorous article "What We Are Doing in Europe," for a 1922 edition of *Vanity Fair*, moreover, reported among other examples as follows: "At Zurich, a marionette theatre has lately produced a play which has caused a real sensation"[37] [fig. 4]. In their anthology of *The Isms of Art* (1925), El Lissitzky and Jean Arp chose to have Dadaism represented by the figure of the Guards[38] [fig. 5]. Finally, in 1929, the Belgian avant-garde magazine *Variétés* reproduced the Guards as part of an image sequence titled "Idols."[39]

To the avant-garde artists, Sophie Taeuber-Arp's marionettes were first and foremost sculptures.[40] Gabrielle Buffet-Picabia, for example, wrote an essay titled "Matières plastiques" for the magazine *XXe siècle* (1938) in which she showed the figure of Freudanalytikus alongside sculptures by Alexander Archipenko, Marcel Duchamp, Pablo Picasso, Francis Picabia, and Man Ray.[41] In the catalogue raisonné of 1948, Hugo Weber listed the marionettes under "Sculpture" as "créations plastiques étonnamment originales."[42] Walter Serner, meanwhile, writing in his Dadaist manifesto *Letzte Lockerung*, defined sculpture as "very unwieldy toys, aggravated by metaphysical eyelashes."[43] The wood-turning technique had a long tradition in the field of toys, while Taeuber-Arp innovatively transferred it to marionettes. The first mention of this was in the 1939 catalogue of *Contemporary Sculpture*, a show conceived by Marcel Duchamp and held at the Guggenheim Jeune Gallery in London. "At the Zurich Exhibition in 1918," wrote the author, "her marionettes in turned wood were the starting point for a new technique in decorative art."[44]

20

DADA

30

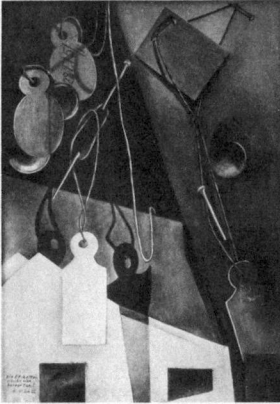

HÖCH
1922

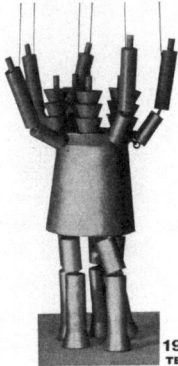

74   1918
TEUBER

1 Parts of this text are a revised and expanded version of an essay published in 2021 as "Interplay of the Arts on Stage: The *King Stag* Marionettes and Stage Sets," in Anne Umland and Walburga Krupp (eds.), *Sophie Taeuber-Arp. Living Abstraction*, exh. cat. The Museum of Modern Art, New York 2021, pp. 95–98.

2 Letter from Sophie Taeuber-Arp to the art historian Hans Hildebrandt, June 24, 1927, The Getty Center Archives.

3 Letter from Werner Wolff to Werner Reinhart, July 28, 1918, Winterthurer Bibliotheken, Sammlung Winterthur.

4 Letter from Sophie Taeuber-Arp (see note 2).

5 See Kunstgewerbemuseum der Stadt Zürich (ed.), *Ausstellung von Neuerwerbungen des Museums 1919/1921*, Wegleitungen des Kunstgewerbemuseums der Stadt Zürich, vol. 37, Zurich 1921, p. 18. Acquired from the Swiss Werkbund for 7,000 Swiss francs on October 31, 1919. Reinhart contributed 3,000, while 4,000 was taken from the Kunstgewerbemuseum's auction fund. See *Inventar. 1906–1921*, Museum für Gestaltung Zürich, Decorative Arts Collection / ZHdK.

6 Letter from Werner Wolff to Alfred Altherr, September 1, 1917, Winterthurer Bibliotheken, Sammlung Winterthur.

7 Cf. Alfred Altherr, "Die Geschichte des Marionettentheaters in der Schweiz," in *UNIMA. Hervorragende Puppentheater aller Welt*, no. 3 (1930), pp. 4–6.

8 Alfred Altherr, *Schatten- und Marionettenspiele*, Zurich 1923, pp. 8 and 12.

9 Carl Fischer, *Marionettentheater*, lecture notes, March 11, 1972 at the Museum Bellerive, private collection.

10 Letter from Sophie Taeuber-Arp to Erika Schlegel, September 13, 1912, in Sophie Taeuber-Arp, *Briefe 1905–1914*, vol. 1, ed. Medea Hoch, Walburga Krupp, and Sigrid Schade, Wädenswil 2021, p. 229.

11 The committee was made up of Werner Reinhart as chairman with Alfred Altherr, Henry Bischoff, Albert Isler, Meinrad Lienert, René Morax, Hermann Scherrer, Heinrich Schlosser, Sophie Taeuber-Arp, and Werner Wolff.

12 Cf. the minutes of the meetings of the Marionettes Committee of October 31, 1917 and January 30, 1918, Stadtarchiv Zürich.

13 Cf. letter from Werner Reinhart to Johanna Fülscher, January 31, 1918, Winterthurer Bibliotheken, Sammlung Winterthur.

14 Cf. Novalis, *Werke*, ed. Gerhard Schulz, Munich 1981, p. 491.

15 Letter from Sophie Taeuber-Arp to Erika Schlegel, March 8, 1919, in Sophie Taeuber-Arp, *Briefe 1917–1928*, vol. 2, ed. Medea Hoch, Walburga Krupp, and Sigrid Schade, Wädenswil 2021, p. 62.

16 "Den II. Teil von Gozzi werden R. Morax und W. Wolff gemeinsam umarbeiten" ("R. Morax and W. Wolff will together rework Gozzi Part II"). Minutes of the Marionettes Committee for the Swiss Werkbund exhibition in Zurich in 1918, January 15, 1918, Stadtarchiv Zürich. What the designation "Part II" actually refers to here is not clear, since in the end the whole play was reworked.

17 See Georges Duplain, *L'homme aux mains d'or. Werner Reinhart, Rilke et les créateurs de Suisse romande*, Lausanne 1988, p. 29.

18 Letter from René Morax to Werner Reinhart, March 11, 1918, Winterthurer Bibliotheken, Sammlung Winterthur.

19 On February 21, 1918, René Morax wrote to Werner Reinhart to inform him that he had finished his updated version of the work and would send it to Werner Wolff for further reworking. Cf. ibid.

20 Cf. letter from Werner Wolff to Werner Reinhart, 27 February 1918, Winterthurer Bibliotheken, Sammlung Winterthur.

21 The French version has Tartaglia tell Angela: "C'est assez bardeé; remplissez vos devoirs conjugaux, mon épouse; au lit, venez au lit" ("That's enough chatter; fulfill your marital duties, wife; to bed, come to bed") III, 1. In the German version, by contrast, he says: "Genug geschwatzt! Erfülle deine Pflicht." ("Enough chatter! Do your duty.") III, 8. Wolff frequently tightened up the French.

22 *King Stag*, Act 2, Scene 4: "The Parrot: I'm so great […] truth"; Act 3, Scene 9: "Freudanalytikus: When all is driven to destruction […] truth"; Act 3, final scene: "Freudanalytikus: And should you not know […] tune!"

23 Carl Fischer in conversation with Gusti Gysin, July/August 1981, privately owned tape recording.

24 Ibid.

25 Letter from Jean Arp to Hans Richter, August 31, 1949, Hans Richter Papers, B.VII.3. The Museum of Modern Art Archives, New York.

26 Katherine S. Dreier and Marcel Duchamp, *Collection of the Société Anonyme: Museum of Modern Art 1920*, New Haven 1950, p. 69.

27 Hans Arp, "Tibiis canere (Zurich, 1915–1929)," in *XXe siècle*, no. 1 (March 1938), pp. 41–44, here p. 42.

28 Max Bill, "Sophie Taeuber-Arp," in *Das Werk*, no. 6 (June 1943), pp. 167–171, here p. 167.

29 There are also ink drawings of the "King's Cabinet" and the tree motif, as well as collages in the original size.

30 Fondation Arp, Clamart.

31 Waldemar Jollos, "Vom Marionettentheater," in *Das Werk*, no. 8 (August 1918), pp. 128–132, here pp. 131–132.

32 h. s., "Marionettentheater," in *Neue Zürcher Zeitung*, September 13, 1918, p. 2.

33 *Züricher Post*, September 11, 1918.

34 k., "Marionetten," in *Neue Zürcher Zeitung*, March 24, 1920, p. 2.

35 gt., "Marionetten-Theater Münchner Künstler," in *Züricher Post*, March 25, 1920.

36 Otto Flake, "Neue Marionetten. Aus dem Marionettentheater des Zürcher Werkbunds," in *Die Dame*, no. 8 (1919), p. 2.

37 Tristan Tzara, "What We Are Doing in Europe," in *Vanity Fair*, no. 1 (September 1922), pp. 68 and 100, here p. 68.

38 Jean Arp mentioned this in "Sophie Taeuber," in *Unsern täglichen Traum … Erinnerungen und Dichtungen aus den Jahren 1914–1954*, Zurich 1955, p. 18: "At El Lissitzky's request, such a marionette depicting a soldier and a whole army all at once appeared in the 'Isms,' too. Lissitzky's interest in theater and figures probably influenced this choice."

39 "Idoles," in *Variétés. Revue mensuelle illustrée de l'esprit contemporain*, no. 9 (January 1929).

40 Véra Idelson, "Problèmes du théâtre moderne," in *Cercle et Carré*, no. 2 (April 1930).

41 Cf. Gabrielle Buffet-Picabia, "Matières plastiques," in *XXe siècle*, no. 2 (1938), pp. 31–35, here p. 34.

42 Georg Schmidt (ed.), *Sophie Taeuber-Arp*, Basel 1948, p. 125.

43 Walter Serner, *Letzte Lockerung. Manifest Dada*, Hannover/Zurich 1920, p. 7.

44 *Contemporary Sculpture*, exh. cat. Guggenheim Jeune, London 1939.

HANA RIBI

THE ROLE OF COMMEDIA DELL'ARTE IN AVANT-GARDE THEATER AS EVIDENCED BY THE TRAGICOMEDY OF *KING STAG*

Before pondering the role of commedia dell'arte in avant-garde theater, taking Carlo Gozzi's tragicomedy *King Stag* as an example, we first have to arrive at a clear understanding of what commedia dell'arte actually was, and which aspects of that theatrical heritage were of most interest to twentieth-century European theater. Reviewing this chapter in the history of theater is essential to a proper appreciation of how the printed Italian original of Gozzi's *Il re cervo* of 1772 differed from René Morax and Werner Wolff's adaptation, *König Hirsch* (*King Stag*) of 1918, and of which historical contexts had an impact on the version for puppet theater. This in turn will provide at least the beginnings of an answer to the question of what led to the revival of the commedia dell'arte tradition in avant-garde puppet theater.

THE COMMEDIA DELL'ARTE TRADITION

Commedia dell'arte is a form of improvisational comedy that from the mid-sixteenth to the late eighteenth century was performed both on Italian piazzas and by itinerant Italian theater companies touring other European cities. The comedians worked with masks with fixed typologies and with improvisation that included pantomime, music, singing, dancing, and circus acts. Every performance had comic interludes that often relied on gags. The acting was characterized by exaggerated gestures, while the language was full of flowery superlatives and hyperbolic escalations of both action and reaction. Commedia dell'arte did not work with scripts but rather with loose sequences of scenes in which ad-libbing actors spoke in their own regional dialects and in all registers, ranging from folk wit to obscenities, including the slang specific to certain social classes. The unique character of this form of theater is reflected in the Italian terms used to denote the old *commedia italiana*.[1] Thus there was talk of *commedia all'improvviso* (impro theater), *commedia a soggetto* (sketches), *commedia delle maschere* (masques), *commedia degli zanni* (comedy of the Zanni), and *commedia dei buffoni* (comedy of fools). The Zanni masks represented the servants who were in the service of the elders (*vecchi*) Pantalone and Dottore, both of whom were figures of ridicule. The Zanni were important drivers of those burlesque scenes in which either the wealthy but gullible Pantalone or the ostensibly erudite and garrulous Dottore went chasing after the maids, only to be thwarted by their cunning servants, much to the audience's delight. Each piece generally had two servants who actively advanced the plot. One Zanne was a clever, proactive schemer, while the other was naive, lazy, and foolish, and hence easily manipulated by the former. This, then, was the classic pair of clowns whose gestures and wordplay were both complementary and mutually enhancing. The classic Venetian Zanni were Arlecchino (also called Truffaldino) and the crafty Brighella. Commedia dell'arte worked with specific mask typologies,[2] that is, stock characters clad in recognizable costumes, who with their expansive, stylized gestures treated spectators to a cascade of gags (*lazzi*) replete with both slapstick and wit [fig. 1]. Their antics laden with satirical takes on topical issues owed their existence to the Carnival of Venice, as the only time of year when the otherwise Argus-eyed republic allowed such masked irreverence.

[fig. 1]   Ambrogio Brambilla, *Zanne telling Pantalone how the Zanni hatched from an egg*, engraving, late sixteenth century

CARLO GOZZI'S ATTEMPT
TO MODERNIZE
COMMEDIA DELL'ARTE

Commedia dei buffoni reached its artistic apogee in the late seventeenth century and as the eighteenth century progressed lost much of its sparkle. The stock characters stopped evolving and their forms ossified. The last major playwrights to attempt to breathe new life into the genre were Carlo Goldoni (1707–1793) and Carlo Gozzi (1720–1806).

The nobly born Gozzi placed his faith in oriental fairy tales as a source of new material with which to revive the tradition. Thus in his tragicomedy *Il re cervo*[3] he appropriates motifs from the Persian fable "Histoire du Prince Fadlallah, fils de Bin-Ortoc, Roi de Mousel," and the Tatar fairy tale "Histoire des quatre Sultanes de Citor."[4] Gozzi retained the stylized mask typologies of traditional commedia dell'arte, but supplemented these with some maskless players who acted and gesticulated in a more realistic style. Far from bringing about the intended revival, however, his introduction of characters that did not belong to the traditional commedia dell'arte troupe, his insertion of scripted dialogue in literary high Italian, and the braking effect of the fairy-tale motifs in fact took him even further away from it. Only his very first work, *L'amore delle tre melarance* (The Love for Three Oranges) of 1761, is pure impro comedy. In general, his texts in the high Italian of Tuscany rest on a three-act farce with several extemporized comic scenes. But these are no longer simply pure buffoonery laced with parody and rapid-fire repartee, and the fairy-tale motifs with their sudden reversals of fortune on the contrary have the effect of slackening the overall pace of the piece. The excitement of Gozzi's *fiabe tea-trali* (theatrical fables) derives from their unexpected outcomes, sudden transfigurations, and magic.

THE GERMAN TRANSLATION OF CARLO GOZZI'S *IL RE CERVO* (1777)

The fairy-tale drama *Il re cervo* was premiered by the Sacchi theater company at the Teatro San Samuele in Venice in 1762. The original Italian script went to print ten years later,[5] and a German translation of the same by Friedrich August Clemens Werthes was published as *Der König Hirsch. Ein tragicomisches Märchen für eine Schaubühne, in drey Akten* (The King Stag: A Tragicomic Fairy Tale for the Stage, in Three Acts) in 1777.[6]

Gozzi's *Il re cervo* features the two Venetian Zan-ni: Brigella as cupbearer to King Deramo and Truffaldin as birdcatcher. The prime minister at court is Tartaglia, who has an amusing stammer and is pathologically am-bitious. The second minister is the gullible Pantalon, while Smeraldina (Columbina) plays the part of seduc-tress. These four commedia dell'arte mask typologies, plus Smeraldina who traditionally plays without a mask, are joined by an extended cast of maskless characters that includes the king and peasants.

The entanglements that ensue are rendered inev-itable by the pattern of relationships already in place between the said characters: Clarisse, Tartaglia's daughter, is in love with Pantalon's son Leander, as he is with her; Angela, Leander's sister and Pantalon's daugh-ter, is secretly in love with King Deramo but is also Tartaglia's object of desire; Brigella's sister Smeraldina is supposedly Truffaldin's sweetheart, but is so vain and conceited that she decides to try her luck as a bridal candidate for the king. Clarisse and Leander, like Angela and King Deramo, follow the commedia dell'arte tradition of letting lovers go maskless.

Gozzi's prologue has Cigolotti, servant of the magician Durandarte, explain that he is expecting his long-absent master, who is intending to perform great miracles, to return in the guise of a parrot on January 5, 1762 (the date of the Venice premiere). His servant is to take him to the forest of Ronzislappe near Serendippo, where he will be caught by a birdcatcher, will punish treachery, and will himself be released from the spell that condemned him to the life of a magician. Cigolotti and the magician Durandarte are figures that belong not to commedia dell'arte but to fairy tale; Gozzi adds still more people and animals, including the king's bodyguard, a hunter, some peasants, an old man, a bear, a parrot, and two stags.

The fairy-tale drama consists of three acts and forty-three scenes. The first two acts include four improvised comic interludes in the commedia dell'arte tradition, that is, scenes without any scripted dialogue with no more than a few written hints as to the action so as to give the comedians as much license as possible. Their job is to ratchet up the pace of the piece and to entertain the audience with comic elements. All the ad-libbing is done in Venetian dialect.

In Act 1, King Deramo is trying to find a wife with the aid of a gift from the magician Durandarte, specifically a statue that sees into the potential candidates' hearts and signals to the king whether or not they are answering honestly. Among the women selected for interrogation are Clarisse, Smeraldina, and Angela. One improvised scene had Leander lamenting Clarisse's betrayal and Truffaldin that of Smeraldina, both men believing that they were about to be cuckolded. The climax of this first act is the moment Deramo falls in love with Angela, the sincerity of whose love for him the statue affirms.

Act 2 begins with Minister Tartaglia in a rage after learning that Angela, the woman he has been coveting, is about to become the wife of King Deramo. In this extemporized scene, Smeraldina indicates that she has not entirely lost interest in Truffaldin; he, however, is still sulking and wants nothing more to do with her. During the hunt then organized to celebrate the king's betrothal to Angela, the jealous Tartaglia persuades the king to share his second great secret. Deramo obliges him by metamorphosing into a stag before his very eyes, whereupon the crafty Tartaglia seizes the chance to slip into the lifeless body of the king. When an old man passing by is unable to tell him which way the stag fled, Tartaglia cruelly kills him on the spot. Meanwhile, Deramo, now a stag, returns to the site of his transfiguration. Unable to find his own body, he dons that of the slain old man instead. The improvised scene that follows has Truffaldin, out catching birds in the forest, chance on a slain stag with a distinctive white spot. The dramatic irony of this scene derives from the fact that the birdcatcher knows nothing of the old man's tragic death or the no less tragic transformation of the king, whereas the audience has witnessed both. Delighted with his find, Truffaldin's only concern now is to slay the beast and claim the reward for "the stag with the white spot" promised by "Deramo," a.k.a. Tartaglia. In the next unscripted scene, Truffaldin does indeed catch the parrot, that is, the magician Durandarte who has been waiting for him. Suddenly, however, he hears a voice calling his name: "Truffaldin!"[7] The birdcatcher goes searching for the voice in the bushes and there, to his horror, discovers the lifeless body of Tartaglia left behind when the prime minister donned Deramo's guise. "Truffaldin, fear not!" says the voice emanating from the parrot. "Carry me to the court of the queen. [...] You shall become rich, rich, rich."[8]

In Act 3, a clap of thunder has the parrot turn back into the magician Durandarte, whereupon everything takes a turn for the better. The king has his body restored to him and the treacherous minister Tartaglia receives his comeuppance by being turned into an old man. Angela falls into Deramo's arms, Clarisse is consoled by Leander, and Pantalon once again understands nothing. Durandarte condemns Tartaglia to die of shame in a public square. "I can already feel remorse and shame gnawing away at my despised life. [...] Such ambition... Love... Jealousy made a monster of me. [...] woe is me, for I am as good as dead,"[9] sighs the contrite Tartaglia before falling down dead. Meanwhile, Durandarte is liberated from his life as a magician. Thus the tragicomedy ends with classical catharsis.

TRANSITION TO THE TWENTIETH CENTURY: "THE ART OF THE THEATER"

Late nineteenth-century Europe saw the emergence of a movement against the prevailing performance practice with its penchant for frontal declamations on narrow proscenia against flat, realistically painted backdrops. Theater reformers criticized the imitation of reality on stage and the kind of sets that used perspective views of buildings and landscapes to give the illusion of a three-dimensional space. The visionary Edward Gordon Craig demanded abstract stage sets that dispensed with all perspective painting and decorating and instead espoused a "grand, architectural style" that would open up the stage space and allow it to be played both horizontally and vertically. Some theater devotees saw the return to masked players and stylized movements as a way of overcoming the stagnation that had by then set in [figs. 2–3]. That commedia dell'arte aroused the interest of many reformers is thus not surprising. Its masked players with their extravagant, pantomimic gestures performing in an empty space in a way that was at once stylized and highly expressive made it an inviting field of experimentation for those eager to breathe new life into theater. Among the most important exponents of three-dimensional, abstract, modernist theater were the aforementioned Edward Gordon Craig as well as Adolphe Appia, Émile Jaques-Dalcroze, Jacques Copeau, and Louis Jouvet. French-speaking Switzerland's progressive theater scene was also involved in the trend-setting work being done along the Florence–Geneva–Paris axis. René Morax, for example, opened the popular Théâtre du Jorat in Mézières in 1908, and before long was being counted among the pioneers of francophone stagecraft. Among the plays of his that were staged there was *Le Roi David* (1921), a drama based on the Biblical narrative that won the theater international acclaim and that Arthur Honegger set to music as *Psalm* later that same year. The 1918 [fig. 2]   Title page of Edward Gordon Craig's magazine *The Mask: A Monthly Journal of the Art of the Theatre*, vol. 1, no. 6, August 1908

FULL PAGE PLATE ✐ Isadora Duncan.

Vol. I. N.° 6. ✐ AUGUST ✐ 1908

THE MASK

A MONTHLY JOURNAL OF THE ✐ ART OF THE THEATRE

EUROPEAN & AMERICAN AGENTS.

LONDON. D. J. RIDER 36 St Martin's Court. Charing Cross Road. W. C. ✐ ✐
BERLIN. *SOLE GERMAN AGENT - SCHUSTER & BUFLEB. Nollendorfstrasse 31. W.*
AMSTERDAM. KIRBERGER & KESPER, 134 Rokin.
BUDAPEST. *NAGEL OTTO Museum-Korut, 2*
MOSCOU. "LA BALANCE" Office, Place du Théâtre
PHILADELPHIA. U. S. A. " THE BUTTERFLY " Office, 1126 Walnut Street.
FLORENCE. 2 *LUNG' ARNO ACCIAIUOLI.*

✐ PRICE ONE SHILLING, NET MONTLY ✐

[fig. 3]   Edward Gordon Craig, mask,
           woodcut, ca. 1911

puppet-play adaptation of *King Stag* by René Morax and Werner Wolff built on these experiments with a commedia dell'arte-style staging and an ensemble of abstract marionettes designed by Sophie Taeuber-Arp.

The commedia dell'arte stock characters are clearly related to those of hand-puppet shows such as Pulcinella, Kasper, and Punch and Judy, as well as the crude slapstick of fairground puppetry. The imperative incumbent on all the artists involved in these experimental productions—many of them influenced by the prominence given to Craig and Appia at the *Theaterkunst* exhibition at the Kunstgewerbemuseum Zurich (Museum of Arts and Crafts, now Museum für Gestaltung Zürich) in 1914—echoed Craig's Art of the Theater: mere imitations of human theater were to be avoided at all costs, while the stylized art of modernist marionette design, duly stripped of all naturalistic trimmings and props, was to be promoted.

KÖNIG HIRSCH BY RENÉ MORAX AND WERNER WOLFF (1918)

Morax's French reworking of *King Stag*, which Wolff expanded on and translated into German,[10] was written specially for a puppet-theater production to be performed at the Swiss Werkbund exhibition in Zurich in 1918. The spark of inspiration for his adaptation of this tragicomic, theatrical fable was Dadaistic in the truest sense of the term. In Morax's retelling, therefore, all the love entanglements and transformations rest on the magic of the secret power of the "Urlibido," over which the magician Freudanalytikus (Durandarte) and his pupil Doctor Oedipus Complex (Cigolotti) have mastery.

Morax thus places the drama on a psychoanalytic footing," turning Gozzi's tale into what is essentially a parody of Freud's libido theory. Not only does this conceit enable him to ramp up the erotic tension already present in the plot, but it also opens up scope for sarcasm and irony. As a doctor's son, a poet, and a man of the theater, Morax undoubtedly knew about Freudian psychoanalysis and put that knowledge to dramatic use in the most amusing way.

The magician Freudanalytikus (Sigmund Freud) is given a servant as sidekick—actually a Faustian and Wagnerian motif—who goes by the name of Doctor Oedipus Complex (C. G. Jung). As in Gozzi, the play opens with the servant awaiting the arrival of his master-turned-parrot, and the date is again that of the planned premiere of the piece in Zurich: May 15, 1918.[12] Doctor Complex tells of the "potent magical mysteries" that Freudanalytikus has entrusted to the King of Serendippo, one of which is a magical apparatus for analyzing the female mind, rather like the speaking statue in Gozzi's play. The parody of Freud and his no less famous pupil Jung is made transparent in the prologue spoken by Doctor Complex: "I must nevertheless admit that despite having long had the honor of being in the service of the great magician Freudanalytikus, I have never truly understood his high teachings. But he did once say to me: My son, beware! Never to speak to anyone of the secrets that I entrusted to the King of Serendippo in the year 1913."[13] [pp. 129 f.] The audience would have understood this reference very well, 1913 having been the year when Freud and Jung fell out over a difference of opinion on the function of the libido. That the magician's second closely guarded secret is the power of the

"Urlibido" is therefore only logical. Presumably it was Jung's conflict with the authority-figure Freud that prompted Morax to give his character in *King Stag* the name Doctor Oedipus Complex.

The issues addressed by the play extend beyond psychoanalysis, however, and include both the First World War and its economic repercussions—the sky-rocketing coal and food prices, for example. Local color is provided by the mention of Zurich landmarks such as the Hotel Bellevue [p. 129] and the Burghölzli forest [pp. 130 and 154], and the provocative remarks on de-serters, defrauders, socialists, and Dadaists scattered throughout the script would undoubtedly have amused the premiere audience. Such sarcastic interjections into a fairy tale about a king and his scheming courtier would have chimed well with the zeitgeist of a period scarred by war and now riven by hardship, Dadaist deserters, and the ever-louder stirrings of the socialist labor move-ment, which within weeks of the premiere would call a general strike.

Morax's reworking of the play in three acts and thirty-six scenes is seven scenes shorter than the origi-nal version by Gozzi and replaces Gozzi's scenes of im-provised commedia dell'arte with witty repartee. One of the most crucial cuts made to the Italian original is that in Act 2, Scene 7, when the king, who is out hunting in the forest, is transformed into a stag. Whereas Gozzi then had him turned into an old man, Morax leaves him as a stag (at least until his human body is restored to him) and by doing so renders obsolete both Tartaglia's brutal murder of the old man and Deramo's magical metamorphosis from stag to old man. Another significant change is Morax's replacement of Gozzi's long-winded restoration scene with a swift and unambiguous denouement.[14] The decision to shorten this episode and to forgo any sudden reversals of fortune tells of Morax's sure feel for the different rules governing puppet theater. After all, he was following the material logic of a puppet in the form of an animal figure, which, as he well knew, was bound to be more convincing than a human actor dressed up as a beast in a conventional staging.

At the end of the play, Morax has the miscreant Tartaglia, clad in a tattered shirt, cry out: "I am naked, my libido visible far and wide [...] Kill me, kill me! I did not analyze myself and can no longer do it now. So kill me!"[15] [p. 182] Freudanalytikus then concludes the performance with the words: "Farewell, and do not forget what you have just seen. Do not leave it too late with analysis! Do not leave it too late to dance to this tune!"[16] [p. 183] The play thus ends with a psychoanalytic catharsis and a recommendation to seek therapy.

The rapid spread of the Spanish flu in the months immediately after the war limited the number of times the play could be performed at the Swiss Werkbund exhibition of 1918 (see the essay by Medea Hoch, p. 188). Not even the restaging of the work undertaken by Paul Brann in the recently founded Schweizerisches Marionettentheater (Swiss Puppet Theater) two years later was able to hold its own in the repertoire. As a well-known director of puppet theater, Brann was accustomed to working with classical marionettes. He had no experience of handling abstract figures, some of them without any joints at all and held together only by brass eye bolts, and found Taeuber-Arp's puppets alien. The desired mobility aesthetic of marionettes called for their movements to be controllable and not merely the

product of brass eye bolts moving in arbitrary directions. This, incidentally, was also the position taken by Carl Fischer, a puppet-maker, woodcarver, and teacher in the arts and crafts department of Zurich's Gewerbeschule (Trade School).

While the experimental marionettes designed by Taeuber-Arp did make it into the limelight as showpieces at major international exhibitions, the script of *King Stag* was left languishing in the archives for more than seven decades and not until 1993 was an attempt made to reconstruct the puppet-theater version of the play. That staging, directed by Claudine Rajchman and Jean-Pierre Bitterli at the Zürcher Puppen Theater (later the Theater Stadelhofen) in collaboration with the Schauspielakademie, presented the work in the sardonic, witty, and wonderfully inventive version by Morax [fig. 4]— much to the delight of the largely local audience.

The reconstruction showed quite clearly that "the spoken text in conjunction with the forms and colors of the abstract marionettes moving against a backdrop of abstract, colorful stage sets gives rise to a synaesthetic symphony of words, forms, colors, and movements that in turn evokes associative images in space."[17] The experiment to combine modernist theater and commedia dell'arte was a resounding success and remains unparalleled to this day.

1 "Die *Commedia italiana*, die italienische Komödie, die man (frühestens) seit Goldoni *Commedia dell'Arte* zu nennen gewohnt ist," in Rudolf Münz, *Theatralität und Theater. Zur Historiographie von Theatralitätsgefügen*, Berlin 1998, p. 141.

2 There are many variant spellings of the stock characters' names. The first part of this essay will use what is now the standard orthography, whereas the second and third parts will abide by the spellings used in the texts under discussion. The same applies to names of places.

3 "Nel caso di *Re cervo*, Gozzi si serve di due fonti, traendo la traccia della vicenda 'portante' dall'*Histoire du Prince Fadlallah fils de Bin Ortoc, Roi de Mousel* e arricchendola di un episodio tratto dall'*Histoire des quatre sultanes de Citor*," in Valentina Caravaglia, *Carlo Gozzi, Il re cervo. A cura di Valentina Caravaglia, introduzione e commento di Paolo Bosisi*, Letteratura universale, Carlo Gozzi, Le Opere, vol. 4, Venice 2013, p. 13.

4 "Histoire du Prince Fadlallah, fils de Bin-Ortoc, Roi de Mousel," in François Pétis de la Croix, *Les Mille et un jours. Contes persans*, trans. into French by François Pétis de la Croix , vol. 2, Amsterdam: Pierre de Coup 1711–1713, pp. 88–178; published in parallel by Ricoeur, Jombert, Foucault in Paris (1710–1712).
"Histoire des quatre Sultanes de Citor," in [Thomas-Simon Gueullette], *Les Mille et un quart-d'heure. Contes tartares, Ornés de figures en taille-douce*, vol. 2, Paris: André Morin 1730, pp. 348–380; published in parallel by Guillaume Saugrain in Paris (1730), Neaulme in Utrecht (1737), and Chez les Librairies Associés in Paris (1753).

5 Carlo Conte Gozzi, *Opere del Co. Carlo Gozzi*, VIII tomi [Il re cervo è nel primo], Venezia: Colombani, 1772–1774.

6 Carlo Conte Gozzi, *Theatralische Werke von Carlo Gozzi*, trans. from the Italian [by Friedrich August Clemens Werthes], 5 Theile, [Der König Hirsch, Theil 1, pp. 353–477], Bern: bey der Typographischen Gesellschaft, 1777–1779.

7 Ibid., Act 2, Scene 14, p. 435.

8 Ibid., Act 2, Scene 14, pp. 435–436.

9 Ibid., Act III, Scene 12, p. 476.

10 There are two versions of the text. Here in this essay, I shall refer to the German version: Carlo Gozzi, *König Hirsch*, dramaturgically revised by René Morax, trans. from the French and expanded by Werner Wolff, typescript, 1918. Museum für Gestaltung Zürich, Decorative Arts Collection/ZHdK. All quotations that follow are taken from the English translation of the original script provided here on pp. 129–183. The page references in the notes refer to the German original. (French original: Carlo Gozzi, *Le Roi Cerf*, dramaturgically revised by René Morax, typescript, 1918. Museum Rolandseck, Sammlung Arp.)

11 *Vorlesungen zur Einführung in die Psychoanalyse* was a series of lectures given by Sigmund Freud in Vienna between 1915 and 1917, and printed by Hugo Heller, Leipzig/Vienna, 1916–1917, 3 parts.

12 In the event, it had to be postponed owing to the Spanish flu and did not take place until September 1918.

13 Gozzi/Morax/Wolff, *König Hirsch* (see note 10), Act I, pp. 1–2.

14 Other playwrights who reworked *King Stag* made similar cuts, among them Otto Zoff, who rewrote the drama for its Zürcher Schauspielhaus premiere on September 13, 1956, see Otto Zoff, *König Hirsch, Komödie in drei Akten, frei nach Carlo Gozzi*, Vienna 1959. The St. Galler Puppentheater gave guest performances of Zoff's adaptation of the play at Kunsthaus Zürich in November 1966. The production was directed by Hans Hiller and used the original puppets by Sophie Taeuber-Arp. See typescript, sheet 2, Zentralbibliothek Zürich.

15 Gozzi/Morax/Wolff, *König Hirsch* (see note 10), Act 3, p. 21.

16 Ibid., p. 22.

17 Hana Ribi, "Themes and Authors from the 1920s and 1930s at the Schweizerisches Marionettentheater (1918–1936) in Zurich," paper given at the international colloquium "PuppetPlays," October 14–16, 2021, Université Paul Valéry, Montpellier.

CHRISTINA THURNER

HOW THE PUPPETS DANCE
SOPHIE TAEUBER-ARP'S
MARIONETTES
IN THE CONTEXT OF
DANCE HISTORY

The play *King Stag* ends with a speech by Freudanalytikus, who admonishes the audience as follows: "Farewell, and do not forget what you have just seen. Do not
leave it too late with analysis! Do not leave it too late to
dance to this tune!"[1] [p. 183] Although here dance is
used figuratively as a metaphor for psychoanalysis, I
shall take the closing line of this puppet play quite literally in what follows. Of course, none of the figures in
King Stag is actually required to dance, either literally
or metaphorically, and we also know that Sophie
Taeuber-Arp's fellow avant-garde artists apprehended
her marionettes "primarily as sculptures,"[2] that is, as
statuesque rather than moving figures; yet dance they
can, and there are a number of clues that point to a
connection between their dancing and the performing
arts of the period.

Not only is Taeuber-Arp known to have enjoyed
moving her own body,[3] to have been an enthusiastic
dancer, and to have created visual works of art that
were influenced by this passion,[4] but scholars have been
able to identify still more salient factors, such as the
fact that Taeuber-Arp created her marionettes at around
the same time as Rudolf von Laban was developing his
system of dance notation using geometric abstractions
(which admittedly was published only later);[5] then there
is the resemblance of the articulated cast of *King Stag*
to the whole-body masks worn by the Dadaists for their
soirée performances in the 1910s; and the obvious sim-
ilarities between Taeuber-Arp's puppets and the costumes that Oskar Schlemmer famously designed for his
Triadic Ballet.[6] What all these coincidences point to is
the dance that was ingrained in these turned, jointed,
and painted wooden figures with their costumes made

of fabric, feathers, and other décor right from the start. The reference here is not to the gestures set in motion by pulling their strings, as when the script describes Smeraldina as approaching King Deramo with "ridiculously over-the-top bowing and scraping"[7] [p. 144], but rather to the marionettes' capacity for dance deriving from their conception as articulated dolls, from the fact of their having grown out of their creator's knowledge of dance.

To illustrate this, the discussion that follows will posit a connection between the marionettes' motoric potential and Taeuber-Arp's own interest in kinetic modes of expression. The fundamental congruence between Taeuber-Arp's body art and visual art is especially conspicuous in the period during which she created her puppets.[8]

Whereas some contemporaries deemed the marionettes for *King Stag* "much too modern and too daring,"[9] the production was a great success and the "crazy physicality of these figurines" felt to warrant special mention.[10] Later viewers, by contrast, observed that the extent to which the marionettes' limbs could be moved was actually quite limited. The art critic Medea Hoch, for example, notes that the puppets "were hard to control, since many of them had only a few strings."[11]

How should such divergent verdicts be interpreted? How can figures whose range of movement is limited to what the puppetmaster can manipulate nevertheless convey dynamic corporeality? One answer to this lies in the avant-garde approach to the body and to dance of the 1910s, and how Taeuber-Arp translated this into her art. As already mentioned, she herself was active both in Zurich Dadaist circles and in the Ausdruckstanz

(expressionist dance) scene. Indeed, it was actually thanks mainly to Taeuber-Arp that there was a good deal of cross-pollination between these two Zurich-based groups,[12] since not only did she take lessons with the German expressionist dancer Mary Wigman [fig. 1] but she also had personal and professional ties to Rudolf von Laban, Käthe Wulff, Suzanne Perrottet, Clara Walther, and Berthe Trümpy. She and her future husband Jean Arp also collaborated with Dadaist friends such as Hugo Ball, Emmy Hennings, Tristan Tzara, Richard Huelsenbeck, and Marcel Janco. Taeuber-Arp performed in Zurich at the Galerie Dada and at Rudolf von Laban's Schule für Bewegungskunst (School for the Art of Movement), as well as taking part in events hosted by the Lebensreform movement in Ascona and at Monte Verità.[13]

She had been teaching the textiles class at the Zurich Gewerbeschule (Trade School) for two years when, in 1918, the Swiss Werkbund Marionettes Committee, of which she was the only female member, commissioned her to design marionettes and stage sets for the play *King Stag* by René Morax and Werner Wolff for the forthcoming Swiss Werkbund exhibition.[14] In a letter to Jean Arp dating from the spring of that same year and penned hastily in "what little free time I have between lessons" (at Laban's school), she tells him that "life is so hectic I still haven't done any work on the marionettes."[15] Taeuber-Arp was apparently so busy dancing that she scarcely had time to work on her figures. Yet it was precisely her personal experience of dance that was to have a decisive impact on the conception of the marionettes.[16]

Ausdruckstanz, wrote Laban in his book *Die Welt des Tänzers*, is about cultivating what he called a "*tänzerischer Sinn*" ("dancing sense"). By this he meant the

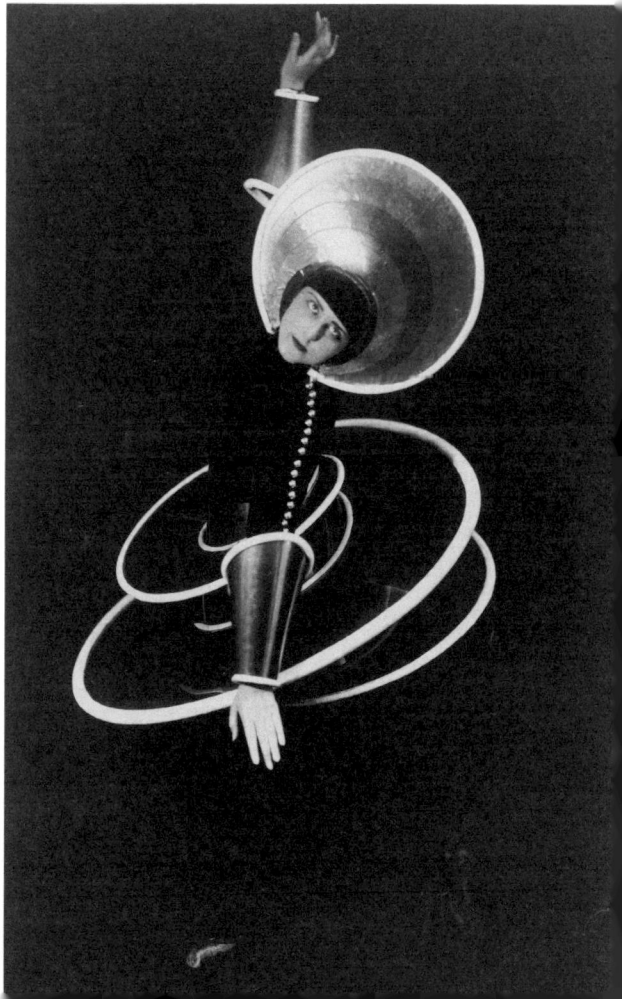

dancer's intuitive ability to translate forms perceived "through the eye and the sense of touch" and "impressions of one's surroundings" into physical movement [fig. 2].[17] It was with such a schooled sensitivity to shapes and their performative potential that Taeuber-Arp designed her marionettes. Each of them is endowed with specific, dynamic, space-shaping properties. The figure of the Guards with its multiple arms, heads, legs, and batons, for example, represents an entire regiment of force. The solid and compact core radiates out into the mobile extremities, becoming ever sharper as it nears the tips of the helmets and the truncheons. The figure of Clarissa, by contrast, is striking on account of her long, willowy limbs, and tutu-like ruffs around the midriff and wrists, the very thought of which prompts the character of Leander to sigh: "She's so delicate, so gentle, so fine!"[18] [p. 139] Meanwhile, Smeraldina, who to Truffaldin seems "so beautiful, so strong, so solid!"[19] [p. 139], embodies a completely different disposition. Her short, stocky legs with their cone-like thighs and much smaller, ellipsoid calves are planted far apart underneath a skirt that flares out from a wasp-like waist. This enables her to walk either on tiptoe or with her feet planted firmly on the ground, whereas lanky, long-legged Clarissa cannot help but stride along, albeit claiming much more space in the process. Thus, certain characteristics are defined for each figure with the result that viewers—assuming they are in possession of a "dancing sense," that is, a schooled eye—can read the shape of the limbs and the arrangement and proportions of the various body parts as indicative of a distinctive motoric potential, even when the marionette is not actually moving at all.

It seems likely that the artist worked according to this principle, albeit in reverse, meaning not receptively but creatively. Having presumably first invented a body to match each character, she then put this body, at least in her imagination, inside a kind of whole-body mask whose potential for movement she proceeded to define and sound out. Taeuber-Arp did not simply transfer movements that she had tried out on her own body to her puppets, but instead was at pains to imagine the characters from the inside out, as it were. In this respect she combined the creative methods of Ausdruckstanz with an understanding of the body and of figures comparable to that of her contemporary Oskar Schlemmer, as evidenced by the sculptural costumes that he created for the dancers in the *Triadic Ballet* [fig. 3]. As the dance researcher and historian Frank-Manuel Peter explains, the dancer in such a costume corpus was "obviously conceived as an 'inner marionette-player.'"[20] Schlemmer, he continues, produced "a marionette in the Kleistian sense" inasmuch as he had creativity and performativity slip into the figure as if into a moving mask, the idea being to make them dance in and with the figure, even if their movements were restricted to whatever the "marionette mechanism" allowed.[21]

That Taeuber-Arp was already familiar with Schlemmer's costumes in 1918 is highly unlikely, especially as most of them were in any case created later.[22] But according to Peter, there can be no doubt that around the middle of the second decade of the century, avant-garde dance artists, among them the Zurich Dadaists, began experimenting with whole-body masks.[23] Ball, for example, praised the "motive power of these masks"[24] and even donned one himself, though he later

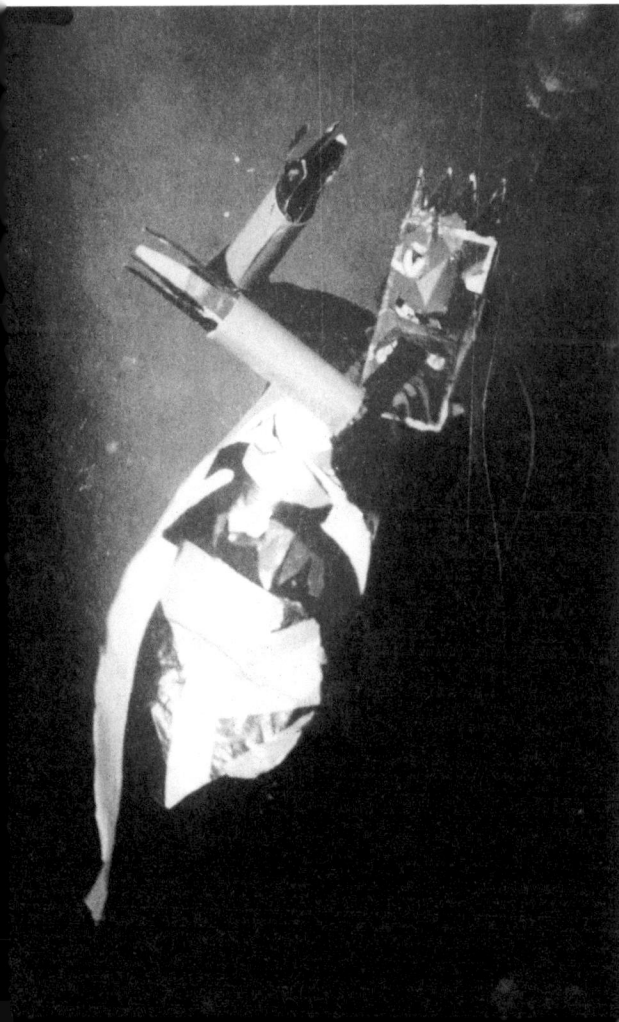

[fig. 4] (Presumably) Sophie Taeuber-Arp
dancing at the opening of the Galerie
Dada in Zurich, 1917

admitted that once inside the costume, he could move only "winglike [...] by raising and lowering my elbows" and since "I could not walk inside the cylinder" had to have himself "carried onto stage in the dark."[25] Taeuber-Arp, too, danced at the Galerie Dada, most likely in a costume and mask designed by Marcel Janco,[26] [fig. 4] whose "lines shattered at her body," wrote Ball, noting that "every gesture is ordered in a hundred parts, sharp, light, pointed."[27] This comment prompted Jean Arp to opine: "What Hugo Ball wrote about Sophie Taeuber-Arp's dance could be repeated with respect to the marionettes that she produced at this time."[28] Their gestures, too, are variously articulated and each of them has its own distinctive quality depending on the motion inscribed into it.

The marionettes for *King Stag* should therefore be viewed in the context of avant-garde dance. Not only are they the products of Taeuber-Arp's "dancing sense," but they actually incorporate dance. When, therefore, the figure of Freudanalytikus concludes *King Stag* by extolling the benefits of psychoanalysis and urging the audience to "dance to this tune"[29] [p. 183], what he is really saying is that it is the marionettes that move people, and not just the other way round.

1   Carlo Gozzi, *König Hirsch*, dramaturgically revised by René Morax, trans. from the French and expanded by Werner Wolff, typescript, 1918, Act 3, p. 22. Museum für Gestaltung Zürich, Decorative Arts Collection/ZHdK. This quotation and those that follow are taken from the English translation of the original script provided here on pp. 129–183. The page references in the notes refer to the German original.

2   Medea Hoch, "Interplay of the Arts on Stage: The *King Stag* Marionettes and Stage Sets," in Anne Umland and Walburga Krupp (eds.), *Sophie Taeuber-Arp. Living Abstraction,* exh. cat. The Museum of Modern Art, New York 2021, pp. 95–98, here p. 97.

3   Sophie Taeuber-Arp in a letter to Jean Arp dated January 23, 1918, in Sophie Taeuber-Arp, *Briefe 1917–1928*, vol. 2, ed. Medea Hoch, Walburga Krupp, and Sigrid Schade, Wädenswil 2021, p. 13: "ich bin froh mich wieder zu bewegen." ("I'm glad to be moving again.")

4   See Sarah Burkhalter, "Kachinas and Kinesthesia: Dance in the Art of Sophie Taeuber-Arp," in Madeleine Schuppli and Aargauer Kunsthaus (eds.), *Sophie Taeuber-Arp. Today is Tomorrow*, Zurich 2014, pp. 226–232.

5   See, both on its own merits and for the reference to Jill Fell (1999), Flora L. Brandl, "On a Curious Chance Resemblance. Rudolf von Laban's Kinetography and the Geometric Abstractions of Sophie Taeuber-Arp," in *Arts*, no. 9 (February 2020), pp. 1–19, here p. 1.

6   Frank-Manuel Peter, *Oskar Schlemmer und der Tanz. Die Tänzernachlässe*, Cologne 2023, pp. 274–275.

7   Gozzi/Morax/Wolff, *König Hirsch* (see note 1), Act 1, p. 16.

8   See Brandl, "On a Curious Chance Resemblance" (see note 5), p. 1; quoted there are pp. 5 and 17, as well as reservations about this assumption.

9   Taeuber-Arp quoted in Hoch, "Interplay of the Arts on Stage" (see note 2), p. 95.

10 Hoch, " Interplay of the Arts on Stage" (see note 2), p. 96.

11 Ibid., p. 97.

12 See Mona De Weerdt and Christina Thurner, "Tanz auf den Dada-Bühnen," in Ursula Amrein and Christa Baumberger (eds.), *dada. Performance & Programme*, Zurich 2017, pp. 106–126.

13 See Mark Franko, "The Choreographic Imaginary: Between Expressionist Dance and Visual Abstraction," in Anne Umland and Walburga Krupp (eds.), *Sophie Taeuber-Arp. Living Abstraction,* exh. cat. The Museum of Modern Art, New York 2021, pp. 92–94, here 92–93.

14 See Hoch, "Interplay of the Arts on Stage" (see note 2), p. 95.

15 Taeuber-Arp, *Briefe 1917–1928* (see note 3), p. 17.

16 See Burkhalter, "Kachinas and Kinesthesia" (see note 4), p. 230, who posits a direct connection between the "tactile knowledge" that Sophie Taeuber-Arp acquired from her "experience as a dancer" and the "construction of the marionettes."

17 Rudolf von Laban, *Die Welt des Tänzers. Fünf Gedankenreigen*, Stuttgart 1920, p. 21.

18 Gozzi/Morax/Wolff, *König Hirsch* (see note 1), Act 1, p. 11.

19 Ibid.

20 Peter, *Oskar Schlemmer und der Tanz* (see note 6), p. 291, where he references the statements of another movement mask artist, Lothar Schreyer.

21 Ibid., p. 278.

22 I have not found any evidence that might convince me otherwise. Peter, too, considers it improbable that Taeuber-Arp would have known of Schlemmer's figurines—and, by the same token, that he would have known of hers—prior to 1918.

23 Peter, *Oskar Schlemmer und der Tanz* (see note 6), p. 279.

24 Hugo Ball, *Flight Out of Time*, Berkeley, Los Angeles, London 1927, p. 64.

25 Ibid, p. 70.

26 See Leah Dickerman, "Object, Mask, Abstraction: The Heads," in Anne Umland and Walburga Krupp (eds.), *Sophie Taeuber-Arp. Living Abstraction*, exh. cat. The Museum of Modern Art, New York 2021, pp. 99–100, here p. 100; see also De Weerdt/Thurner, "Tanz auf den Dada-Bühnen" (see note 12), p. 106.

27 Hugo Ball, "On Occultism, the Hieratic, and Other Strangely Beautiful Things" (1917), trans. Debbie Lewer, *Art in Translation 5*, no. 3 (2013), p. 407.

28 Arp, quoted in Hoch, "Interplay of the Arts on Stage" (see note 2), p. 97.

29 Gozzi/Morax/Wolff, *König Hirsch* (see note 1), Act 3, p. 22.

ASTRID VON ASTEN

"BURLESQUE INVENTIONS"[1]
ON THE PLACE OF THE MARIONETTES IN SOPHIE TAEUBER-ARP'S OEUVRE

Sophie Taeuber-Arp's influence on geometric abstraction as one of the main currents of twentieth-century art was wide-ranging. Just how deeply rooted was her need for orderly arrangements of shapes and a precision-calibrated palette was evident from her early textile designs. The same constructivist language of forms informed the incomparable ensemble of marionettes that she created in 1918 and that went on to become an icon of avant-garde art.

Taeuber-Arp learned a range of craft techniques in the course of her professional training. After passing through conservative educational establishments in St. Gallen, the lessons she attended at the progressive Debschitz School in Munich from 1910 to 1914 ushered in a turning point in her development as an artist. It was at this Lehr- und Versuch-Atelier für angewandte und freie Kunst (Instructional and Experimental Studio for Applied and Fine Art), named for its director Wilhelm von Debschitz, that Taeuber-Arp became proficient in the handling of the most diverse materials. Besides acquiring various textile techniques, she also learned how to use a lathe to turn wood. This was a method that would serve her well in several different phases of her work, including the avant-garde reliefs of the 1930s, whose wooden cones and cylinders she used to explore visual constellations and equilibria in three dimensions. The grounding thus acquired enabled her to tease out each material's intrinsic potential to optimum effect. This kind of design that took its cues from the material came to typify the creations of both the Swiss Werkbund and Das Neue Leben, organizations to which Taeuber-Arp belonged and whose aspiration to see art infuse every area of life she shared.

These two approaches, both of which rested on an implicit connection between artistic ideas and ethical principles, together formed the basis of her art. The avant-garde marionettes are therefore part of an overarching concept, and as such can be either loosely or closely tied to the works that came before and after. Between 1916 and 1918, Taeuber-Arp created a number of turned, goblet-like, wooden receptacles. These objects, and even more so the *Têtes Dada* that she produced in parallel to the marionettes in 1918, show her veering off traditional paths in order to be able to conceptualize more freely. The affinity between the sculptural-looking heads and the marionettes derives from Taeuber-Arp's application of the same methods, including the careful painting of their finely turned surfaces, the glued-on, geometrically protruding noses, and the choice of striking and highly original headdresses [fig. 1]. The connection is made explicit by the titles given to portrait heads such as the one dedicated to Jean Arp: *Study for a Marionette (H. A.).*[2]

The turning of each segment of the marionettes was an innovative alternative to the more traditional practice of carving. For Taeuber-Arp, it was also a way of putting the circle and its abstract derivatives—cones, cylinders, and ovoids—to good use as form-giving elements. It is this ornamental, geometric language of forms that forges the close stylistic affinity between each meticulously formulated countenance and the *Têtes Dada*. Especially impressive is the way she accentuates her puppets' very different temperaments. King Deramo's golden body, for example, is assembled out of harmoniously proportioned cones embellished by a mantle and a magnificent headdress crowning the royal head, which, viewed together, radiate majestic serenity.

[fig. 1]   Sophie Taeuber-Arp, *Head*, turned and
            painted wood, 1918

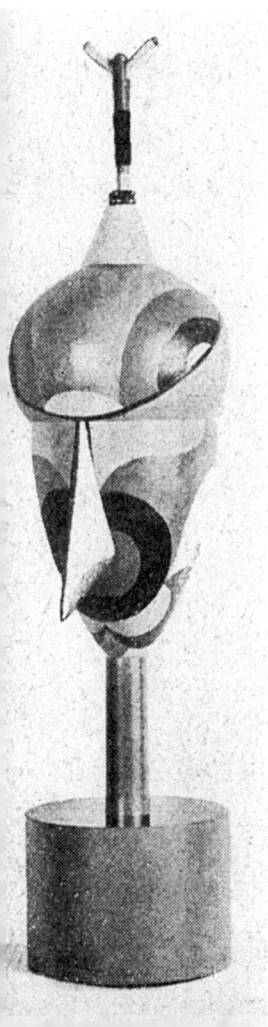

[fig. 2] Sophie Taeuber-Arp, *Märchenmappe*
(Fairy Tale Portfolio), collage, ca. 1918–1920

What a contrast to the wonderful invention of the restless, robotic Guards! As a critic reporting on a performance of the play in 1920 wrote: "How exquisite the impact of those bodyguards, those conjoined people, no longer individuals, more an automaton."3 The deployment of cold silver paint underscores the technoid quality of this figure. The same color, in the form of silver foil, recurs in the stage sets. Indeed, the artist used silver foil in a number of spatial contexts, generally as a means of accentuating certain features. Thus it was silver foil that supplied the gleaming highlights in Taeuber-Arp's wall and ceiling designs for the monumental interior of the Café Aubette in Strasbourg in the second half of the 1920s. In retrospect the stage sets for *King Stag* can therefore be viewed as a pioneering field of experimentation [pp. 34–41]. Otto Flake, in his description of 1919, was the first commentator to capture the atmospheric impression made by them: "Glowing in the soft stage lighting, the space was brought to life by the nuances of red, and the red then canceled out by the silver."4

In one of these fairy-tale stage sets, Taeuber-Arp added trees and mythical creatures as a way of injecting rhythm into the strictly perpendicular grid that is so characteristic of her idiom. The same motifs feature in several works of hers from this period, among them a beaded bag and the so-called *Märchenmappe* (Fairy Tale Portfolio) [fig. 2]. This versatile approach to imagery was fundamental to the artist's working method, especially since by then she had amassed a whole repertoire of abstract-figural subjects to draw on.

There is a surprising affinity with one of the *Duo-Collages* created together with Jean Arp, again in 1918, which also makes use of silver foil. Here, liberated from

all narrative content, the purely geometric structure comes to the fore in all its austere clarity, [fig. 3] allowing it to be read as an early, independent advance towards purely constructivist, concrete art.

The figurines arose at a time when the artist was drawing inspiration from two opposite poles: her teaching at the comparatively traditional Gewerbeschule (Trade School), and the circle of the anarchic Dadaists. The influence of the latter is reflected in the turned heads described above, which, dating from 1920, are essentially a distinct sculptural declaration of allegiance to Dada [fig. 4]. The relationship between the many-limbed, ultra-mobile marionettes and Taeuber-Arp's own expressive dance remains more subtle, although the connection is hinted at in the remarks of Hugo Ball, who, after watching her dance at the opening of the Galerie Dada, saw a "visible effect on the hundred-jointed body"[5] and described the performance as "every gesture is ordered in a hundred parts, sharp, light, pointed"[6] (see the essay by Christina Thurner, pp. 224 ff.). Before long, Taeuber-Arp was flanking the movements she performed in real life with translations of the same into two dimensions. Later, in the mid-1920s, she would vary the theme of bodies with angled arms reaching upwards both in two monumental mural designs—the first for the dance hall of the Hotel Hannong in Strasbourg (1926) [fig. 5] and the second for the foyer and stairwell of the Haus Heimendinger (1928)—or even earlier in her filigree beadwork [fig. 6]. The implied range of (angular) movement recalls the marionette Freudanalytikus and the Statue in the *King Stag* ensemble.

"The artistic consistency of her style warrants the attention of all circles involved in modern art,"[7] wrote

one deeply impressed commentator in the press within hours of the premiere of *King Stag*. Yet the enduring interest in the marionettes taken by avant-garde circles was to prove even more significant in the long run. Writing in pioneering publications such as *Der Zeltweg*,[8] the Dadaists hailed Taeuber-Arp as a great pioneer, while at the same time emphasizing her "artistic audacity."[9] The first compendium of all the myriad avant-garde currents of the early twentieth century, *The Isms of Art*,[10] moreover, featured a photographic reproduction of the Guards attesting to the marionettes' enduring relevance. Taeuber-Arp herself was undoubtedly aware of the significance of these works in shaping public perceptions of her as an artist. She therefore accorded them a prominent place in her album of 1930, whose photos record the evolution of her works between 1916 and 1929. And when she was asked to prepare her entry for the new 1936 edition of the *Schweizerisches Künstler-Lexikon*, she decided to highlight the milestones in her biography as follows: her work as a teacher (1916–1929), her participation in the Dada movement (1918–1920), her murals and interiors (1927–1935), and the marionettes.[11]

1 "Die Figurinen von Frl. Sophie H. Taeuber sind an sich schon burleske Einfälle." ("These figurines by Miss Sophie H. Taeuber are truly burlesque inventions.") In k., "Marionetten," in *Neue Zürcher Zeitung*, March 24, 1920, p. 2. For this and all the other *NZZ* articles cited here, see https://zeitungsarchiv.nzz.ch/archive.

2 *Das neue Leben: erste Ausstellung*, exh. cat. Kunsthalle Basel, Basel 1918, p. 14.

3 k., "Marionetten" (see note 1).

4 Otto Flake, "Neue Marionetten," in *Die Dame*, no. 8, Berlin 1919, p. 2.

5 Hugo Ball, *Flight Out of Time*, ed. John Elderfield and trans. Ann Raimes, Berkeley, Los Angeles, London 1927, p. 102.

6 Hugo Ball, "On Occultism, the Hieratic, and Other Strangely Beautiful Things" (November 15, 1917), trans. Debbie Lewer, *Art in Translation* 5, no. 3 (2013), p. 407.

7 "Lokales," in *Neue Zürcher Zeitung*, September 11, 1918, p. 1.

8 *Der Zeltweg*, ed. Otto Flake, Walter Serner, and Tristan Tzara, Zurich 1919.

9 Waldemar Jollos, "Vom Marionettentheater," in *Das Werk*, no. 8, 1918, p. 131.

10 El Lissitzky and Hans Arp (eds.), *Die Kunstismen / Les Ismes de l'art / The Isms of Art, 1914–1924*, Erlenbach-Zurich / Munich / Leipzig 1925.

11 Correspondence of Wilhelm Wartmann on the planned new edition of the *Schweizerisches Künstler-Lexikon*, June 1936, SIK-ISEA, https://recherche.sikisea.ch.

ENCORE

Altherr, Alfred, "Die Geschichte des Marionettentheaters in der Schweiz," in *UNIMA. Hervorragende Puppentheater aller Welt*, no. 3 (1930), pp. 4–6.

Altherr, Alfred, *Schatten- und Marionettenspiele*, Zurich 1923.

Arp, Hans, "Tibiis canere (Zurich, 1915–1929)," in *XXe siècle*, no. 1 (March 1938), pp. 41–44.

Arp, Hans, "Sophie Taeuber-Arp," in *Unsern täglichen Traum … Erinnerungen und Dichtungen aus den Jahren 1914–1954*, Zurich 1955, p. 18.

Ball, Hugo, *Flight Out of Time*, ed. John Elderfield and trans. Ann Raimes, Berkeley, Los Angeles, London 1927.

Ball, Hugo, *Der Künstler und die Zeitkrankheit. Ausgewählte Schriften*, ed. Hans Burkhard Schlichting, Frankfurt am Main 1984.

Ball, Hugo, "On Occultism, the Hieratic, and Other Strangely Beautiful Things" (November 15, 1917), trans. Debbie Lewer, *Art in Translation 5*, no. 3 (2013), p. 407.

Bill, Max, "Sophie Taeuber-Arp," in *Das Werk*, no. 6 (June 1943), pp. 167–171.

Brandl, Flora L., "On a Curious Chance Resemblance. Rudolf von Laban's Kinetography and the Geometric Abstractions of Sophie Taeuber-Arp," in *Arts*, no. 9 (February 2020), pp. 1–19.

Buffet-Picabia, Gabrielle, "Matières plastiques," in *XXe siècle*, no. 2 (1938), p. 34.

Burkhalter, Sarah, "Kachinas and Kinesthesia: Dance in the Art of Sophie Taeuber-Arp," in Madeleine Schuppli and Aargauer Kunsthaus (eds.), *Sophie Taeuber-Arp. Today is Tomorrow*, Zurich 2014, pp. 226–232.

Caravaglia, Valentina, *Carlo Gozzi, Il re cervo. A cura di Valentina Caravaglia, introduzione e commento di Paolo Bosisio*, Letteratura universale, Carlo Gozzi, Le Opere, vol. 4, Venice 2013.

"Commedia dell'Arte," in: *Theaterlexikon. Teil 1: Begriffe und Epochen*, ed. Manfred Brauneck and Gérard Schneilin, Reinbek 2007, pp. 272–278.

Das neue Leben: erste Ausstellung, exh. cat. Kunsthalle Basel, Basel 1918, p. 14.

De Weerdt, Mona and Christina Thurner, "Tanz auf den Dada-Bühnen," in Ursula Amrein and Christa Baumberger (eds.), *dada. Performance & Programme*, Zurich 2017, pp. 106–126.

Der Zeltweg, ed. Otto Flake, Walter Serner, and Tristan Tzara, Zurich 1919.

Dickerman, Leah, "Object, Mask, Abstraction: The Heads," in Anne Umland and Walburga Krupp (eds.), *Sophie Taeuber-Arp. Living Abstraction*, exh. cat. The Museum of Modern Art, New York 2021, pp. 99–100.

Dreier, Katherine S. and Marcel Duchamp, *Collection of the Société Anonyme: Museum of Modern Art 1920*, New Haven 1950.

Duplain, Georges, *L'homme aux mains d'or. Werner Reinhart, Rilke et les créateurs de Suisse romande*, Lausanne 1988.

El Lissitzky and Hans Arp (eds.), *Die Kunstismen / Les Ismes de l'art / The Isms of Art, 1914–1924*, Erlenbach-Zurich / Munich / Leipzig 1925.

Flake, Otto, "Neue Marionetten. Aus dem Marionettentheater des Zürcher Werkbunds," in *Die Dame*, no. 8 (1919), p. 2.

Franko, Mark, "The Choreographic Imaginary: Between Expressionist Dance and Visual Abstraction," in Anne Umland and Walburga Krupp (eds.), *Sophie Taeuber-Arp. Living Abstraction*, exh. cat. The Museum of Modern Art, New York 2021, pp. 92–94.

Gozzi, Carlo Conte, *Opere del Co. Carlo Gozzi*, VIII tomi [Il re cervo è nel primo], Venezia: Colombani, 1772–1774.

Gozzi, Carlo Conte, *Theatralische Werke von Carlo Gozzi*, trans. Friedrich August Clemens Werthes, 5 Theile, [Der König Hirsch, Theil 1, pp. 353–477], Bern: bey der Typographischen Gesellschaft, 1777–1779.

gt., "Marionetten-Theater Münchner Künstler," in *Züricher Post*, March 25, 1920.

"Histoire des quatre Sultanes de Citor," in [Thomas-Simon Gueullette], *Les Mille et un quart-d'heure. Contes tartares, Ornés de figures en taille-douce*, vol. 2, Paris: André Morin 1730, pp. 348–380.

"Histoire du Prince Fadlallah, fils de Bin-Ortoc, Roi de Mousel," in *Les Mille et un jours. Contes persans*, trans. François Pétis de la Croix, vol. 2, Amsterdam: Pierre de Coup 1711–1713, pp. 88–178.

Hoch, Medea, "Interplay of the Arts on Stage: The *King Stag* Marionettes and Stage Sets," in Anne Umland and Walburga Krupp (eds.), *Sophie Taeuber-Arp. Living Abstraction*, exh. cat. The Museum of Modern Art, New York 2021, pp. 95–98.

h. s., "Marionettentheater," in *Neue Zürcher Zeitung*, September 13, 1918, p. 2.

Idelson, Véra, "Problèmes du théâtre moderne," in *Cercle et Carré*, no. 2 (April 1930).

"Idoles," in *Variétés. Revue mensuelle illustrée de l'esprit contemporain*, no. 9 (January 1929).

Jollos, Waldemar, "Vom Marionettentheater," in *Das Werk*, no. 8 (August 1918), pp. 128–132.

Jung, C. G., "Wandlungen und Symbole der Libido. Beiträge zur Entwicklungsgeschichte des Denkens," in *Jahrbuch für psychoanalytische und psychopathologische Forschungen III. und IV. Band*, Leipzig/Vienna 1912.

k., "Marionetten," in *Neue Zürcher Zeitung*, March 24, 1920, p. 2.

Kotte, Andreas, *Theaterwissenschaft: eine Einführung*, UTB, vol. 2665, Cologne/Weimar/Vienna 2005.

Kratochvíl, Karel, *Ze světa Komedie dell'Arte*, Prague 1987.

Krömer, Wolfram, *Die Italienische Commedia dell'arte* (Erträge der Forschung 62), Darmstadt 1976.

Kunstgewerbemuseum der Stadt Zürich (ed.), *Ausstellung von Neuerwerbungen des Museums 1919/1921*, Wegleitungen des Kunstgewerbemuseums der Stadt Zürich, vol. 37, Zurich 1921.

"Lokales," in *Neue Zürcher Zeitung*, September 11, 1918, p. 1, https://zeitungsarchiv.nzz.ch/archive.

Minges, Klaus, "Staatsbildende Insekten. Sophie Taeubers Marionetten zu 'König Hirsch' im Museum Bellerive Zürich," in *Weltkunst*, November 15, 1996, pp. 2958–2959.

Münz, Rudolf, *Theatralität und Theater. Zur Historiographie von Theatralitätsgefügen*, Berlin 1998.

Museum für Gestaltung Zürich and Sabine Flaschberger (eds.), *Lasst die Puppen tanzen/Turn the Puppets Loose*, Sammeln heisst forschen/Collecting as Research, vol. 3, Zurich 2017.

Novalis, *Werke*, ed. Gerhard Schulz, Munich 1981.

Peter, Frank-Manuel, *Oskar Schlemmer und der Tanz. Die Tänzernachlässe*, Cologne 2023.

Ribi, Hana, *Edward Gordon Craig – Figur und Abstraktion: Craigs Theatervisionen und das Schweizerische Marionettentheater: Die EGC Sammlung im Museum für Gestaltung in Zürich*, ed. Schweizerische Gesellschaft für Theaterkultur, Schweizer Theaterjahrbuch, vol. 61, Basel 2000.

Riha, Karl, *Commedia dell'arte. Mit den Figurinen Maurice Sands*, Frankfurt am Main 1980.

Roth, Klaus and Erich Lück: "Die Saccharin-Saga. Ein Molekülschicksal," in *Chemie in unserer Zeit*, no. 45 (2011), Weinheim 2011, pp. 406–423, doi:10.1002/ciuz.201100574.

Schlemmer, Oskar, "L.H.M. Es ist hohe Zeit Ihnen zu schreiben. Brief an Otto Meyer-Amden," August 7, 1920, https://www.staatsgalerie.de/de/sammlung-digital/lhm-es-hohe-zeit-ihnen-schreiben.

Schmidt, Georg (ed.), *Sophie Taeuber-Arp*, Basel 1948.

Serner, Walter, *Letzte Lockerung. Manifest Dada*, Hannover/Zurich 1920.

Spörri, Reinhart, *Die Commedia dell'arte und ihre Figuren*, reihe schau-spiel 4, Wädenswil 1977.

Taeuber-Arp, Sophie, *Briefe 1905–1914*, vol. 1, ed. Medea Hoch, Walburga Krupp, and Sigrid Schade, Wädenswil 2021.

Taeuber-Arp, Sophie, *Briefe 1917–1928*, vol. 2, ed. Medea Hoch, Walburga Krupp, and Sigrid Schade, Wädenswil 2021.

Taeuber-Arp, Sophie, *Briefe 1929–1942*, vol. 3, ed. Medea Hoch, Walburga Krupp, and Sigrid Schade, Wädenswil 2021.

Thurner, Christina, "Bewegung zur Disposition. Dada und die Tanzreform," in Mona De Weerdt and Andreas Schwab (eds.), *Monte Dada. Ausdruckstanz und Avantgarde*, Bern 2017, pp. 30–41.

Tzara, Tristan, "What We Are Doing in Europe," in *Vanity Fair*, vol. 19, no. 1 (September 1922), pp. 68 and 100, https://archive.vanityfair.com/issue/19220901/print.

Umland, Anne and Walburga Krupp (eds.), *Sophie Taeuber-Arp. Living Abstraction*, exh. cat. The Museum of Modern Art, New York 2021.

von Laban, Rudolf, *Die Welt des Tänzers. Fünf Gedankenreigen*, Stuttgart 1920.

Wegner, Manfred (ed.), *Handbuch zum Künstlerischen Puppenspiel 1900–1945: Deutschland, Österreich, Schweiz*, Munich 2019.

Züricher Post, September 11, 1918.

SABINE FLASCHBERGER studied history and history of art at the University of Zurich and has been curator of the Decorative Arts Collection at the Museum für Gestaltung Zürich since 2011. There she is responsible for exhibitions and publications at the interface of the decorative arts, fine arts, and design. Among the exhibitions that she has curated are: *The Empire of Folds: Fashion and Textile Art from Japan* (2013), *Mucha Manga Mystery* (2013), *Say It with Flowers* (2014), *Cose Fragili—Murano Glass* (2015), *The Textile Room* (2015), *Turn the Puppets Loose* (2017), *Énergie animale* (2020), *Atelier Zanolli—Fabrics, Fashion, Craft 1905–1939* (2022), and *Textile Manifestos—From Bauhaus to Soft Sculpture* (2025).

SOPHIE GROSSMANN studied cultural publishing at Zurich University of the Arts and history of art at the University of Bern, where she specialized in the history of textile arts. In 2022 she became a research associate at the Museum für Gestaltung Zürich, where her focus is on the museological questions raised by collecting born-digital and hybrid objects as well as the history of the institutional practice of collecting and exhibiting decorative arts objects. Another important field of research for her is the cross-pollination of fashion and the performing arts in the early twentieth century.

MEDEA HOCH is an art critic and curator whose interdisciplinary interests mainly have to do with modernism and contemporary art. As a researcher at the Institute for Cultural Studies in the Arts at Zurich University of the Arts, she received funding from the Swiss National Fund to study Sophie Taeuber-Arp's puppet play *King Stag* and the interactions of different disciplines in the work of that pioneer of abstract art. Among her numerous publications on Sophie Taeuber-Arp are three that she co-authored: *Sophie Taeuber-Arp. Briefe 1905–1942* (2021), *Sophie Taeuber-Arp*, a guide to the eponymous exhibition at the Tate Modern in London (2021), and *Sophie Taeuber. Textilreformerin* (2024).

JULIA KLINNER studied history of art and general and comparative literary studies at the University of Zurich. She has been a registrar of the Decorative Arts Collection of the Museum für Gestaltung Zürich since 2018. As a research associate there since 2024, she also engages in provenance research and investigates the historical contexts and origin stories of the objects in the collection.

HANA RIBI did her doctorate at the Institute of Theatre Studies at the University of Bern. Her principal field of research is the theory and practice of puppet theater. She was the co-founder and first director of the Zürcher Puppen Theater (now the Theater Stadelhofen). She writes, directs, organizes international exhibitions, and publishes on questions relating to puppet theater. Her creative work includes designing the puppets for Pablo Picasso's play *Desire Caught by the Tail* (1986), which she also directed. The 2004 exhibition catalog *Metamorphosen – Hana Ribi – Theater in progress* provides information on her work. She is the author of monographs entitled *Fred Schneckenburgers Puppencabaret* (1991) and *Edward Gordon Craig – Figur und Abstraktion* (2000), as well as a contributor to *Turn the Puppets Loose* (2017) and *Handbuch zum Künstlerischen Puppenspiel 1900–1945* (2019), among others.

CHRISTINA THURNER is Professor for Dance Studies at the Institute of Theatre Studies at the University of Bern. Her research interests include the history and aesthetics of dance from the eighteenth century to the present, contemporary dance and performance, historiography, dance criticism, and autobiographical research. Her most recent publications are *Erinnerungen tanzen. Autobiografien als Quellen der Tanzhistoriografie* (2024) and *Theater und Tanz. Handbuch für Wissenschaft und Studium* (2023), which she co-edited with Beate Hochholdinger-Reiterer and Julia Wehren.

ASTRID VON ASTEN has been a curator of the art of Hans Arp and Sophie Taeuber-Arp at the Arp Museum Bahnhof Rolandseck since 2000. One of her principal research interests is the avant-garde art of the early twentieth century. She is the author of numerous catalog texts and academic papers, and provided curatorial support for the installation of the museum's new wing. Since then she has conceived a range of exhibitions that show the work of Arp and Taeuber-Arp in their larger artistic context, including *Genese Dada* (2016), *Kosmos Arp* (2023), and *Netzwerk Paris— Abstraction-Création—1931–1937* (2025).

1   Sophie Taeuber-Arp, stage set design for *King Stag*, wax crayon and pencil on paper, cardboard, 9.6 × 16.4 cm, 1918. Stiftung Arp e. V., Berlin/Rolandswerth

3   Sophie Taeuber-Arp, stage set design for *King Stag*, wax crayon and pencil on paper, cardboard, 10.1 × 16.3 cm, 1918. Stiftung Arp e. V., Berlin/Rolandswerth

5   Sophie Taeuber-Arp, stage set design for *King Stag*, wax crayon on paper, cardboard, 8.4 × 13.2 cm, 1918. Museum für Gestaltung Zürich, Graphics Collection/ZHdK

7   Sophie Taeuber-Arp, stage set design for *King Stag*, wax crayon and pencil on paper, cardboard, 9.5 × 16.5 cm, 1918. Museum für Gestaltung Zürich, Graphics Collection/ZHdK

17   Photo: Ernst Linck, Zurich. Familienarchiv Jung, Küsnacht

19   Photo: G. Abegg © Fondation Arp

20   Photo: J. P. Pichon © Fondation Arp

23   Photo: Ernst Linck, Zurich. Stiftung Arp e. V., Berlin/Rolandswerth

24, 221   Photo: unknown. Museum für Gestaltung Zürich, Decorative Arts Collection/ZHdK

31, 32, 122–125   Museum für Gestaltung Zürich, Decorative Arts Collection/ZHdK

34–41   Photo: Ernst Linck, Zurich. Zurich University of the Arts, Archive ZHdK. The quotations by Sophie Taeuber-Arp are taken from the backs of prints of the same photograph from the Fondation Arp.

46–125   Sophie Taeuber-Arp (design/painting), marionettes for *King Stag*, assembled by Carl Fischer, 1918. Pedestal for the Statue replicated by Mel Myland and Sabine Gysin, 1993. Photo: U. Romito & I. Šuta, Museum für Gestaltung Zürich/ZHdK. Museum für Gestaltung Zürich, Decorative Arts Collection/ZHdK

189   Museum für Gestaltung Zürich, Poster Collection/ZHdK © Hugo Stüdeli, Solothurn

190   Photo: Ernst Linck, Zurich. Zurich University of the Arts, Archive ZHdK

192   Museum für Gestaltung Zürich, Poster Collection/ZHdK © Carl und Margrit Roesch-Stiftung Diessenhofen

201   Tristan Tzara Estate

203   Photo: Ernst Linck, Zurich. In: El Lissitzky, Hans Arp, *Die Kunst-ismen/Les Ismes de l'art/The Isms of Art, 1914–1924*, Erlenbach-Zurich/Munich/Leipzig 1925, p. 20. Museum für Gestaltung Zürich, Graphics Collection/ZHdK © 2025 ProLitteris, Zurich

208   Collection Fossard, National Museum Stockholm

215, 216   Bibliothèque nationale de France, Paris © Edward Gordon Craig Estate. All rights reserved. Used with permission

227   Photo: Ernst Linck, Zurich (presumably). SIK-ISEA, Zurich (reproduction: Philippe Hitz)

229   Photo: unknown © fine art images

230   Photo: Karl Grill. Deutsches Tanzarchiv Köln © 2025. Digital image, The Museum of Modern Art, New York/Scala, Firenze

233   Photo: unknown. Stiftung Arp e.V., Berlin/Rolandswerth

239   In *Das Neue Leben*, exh. cat. Kunsthaus Zürich, Zurich 1919. Kunsthaus Zürich, Bibliothek

240   Photo: Brigitt Lattmann. Aargauer Kunsthaus Aarau/Depositum aus Privatbesitz

242   bpk/Nationalgalerie, SMB/Jörg P. Anders © 2025, ProLitteris, Zurich

244   bpk/CNAC-MNAM/Georges Meguerditchian

245   Fondation Arp

246   Photo: Marlen Perez, Museum für Gestaltung Zürich/ZHdK. Museum für Gestaltung Zürich, Decorative Arts Collection/ZHdK

We have made every effort to locate all copyright holders. Copyright holders not mentioned in the credits are asked to substantiate their claims, and recompense will be made according to standard practice.

**Museum
für Gestaltung
Zürich**

*King Stag
Carlo Gozzi's Tragicomedy in a
Staging for Marionettes by
Sophie Taeuber-Arp, René Morax,
and Werner Wolff*

A Publication of the Museum für
Gestaltung Zürich
    Christian Brändle, Director

Editors: Museum für Gestaltung
    Zürich, Sabine Flaschberger,
    Petra Schmid
Concept and editing:
    Sabine Flaschberger, Petra Schmid
Design: Hubertus Design, Zurich;
    Kerstin Landis, Jonas Voegeli
Photography:
    Umberto Romito, Ivan Šuta
Project management publisher:
    Chris Reding
Scientific and editorial collaboration:
    Sophie Grossmann, Julia Klinner
Translations: Bronwen Saunders
Copy editing: Sarah Quigley
Proofreading: Colette Forder
Image research: Regula Kreis
Image processing: Seraphin GmbH
Printing and binding: DZA Druckerei
    zu Altenburg GmbH, Thuringia
Paper: Munken Lynx Rough, Olin
    Design Smooth ultimate white,
    Transphère green, Gmund Color
Typeface: Reply, Letter Gothic

Verlag Scheidegger & Spiess AG
Niederdorfstrasse 54
8001 Zurich, Switzerland
www.scheidegger-spiess.ch
+41 44 262 16 62
info@scheidegger-spiess.ch

Product safety
Responsible person pursuant to EU
    Regulation 2023/988 (GPSR):
GVA Gemeinsame Verlagsauslieferung
    Göttingen GmbH & Co. KG
Post Box 2021
37010 Göttingen, Germany
T +49 551 384 200 0
E info@gva-verlage.de

Scheidegger & Spiess is being
    supported by the Federal Office of
    Culture with a general subsidy for
    the years 2021–2025.
ISBN 978-3-03942-274-6

German edition
ISBN 978-3-03942-273-9

Z
The museum of
Zurich University of the Arts
zhdk.ch

Museum für Gestaltung Zürich
Ausstellungsstrasse 60
P. O. Box
8031 Zurich, Switzerland
www.museum-gestaltung.ch